Border Voices 14

Verbal fireworks, prosodic pyrotechnics, and even a METAPHOR or two ... by San Diego students and acclaimed guest poets Adrienne Rich, Robert Pinsky, Catherine Yi-yu Cho Woo and Steve Kowit.

ISBN, BORDER VOICES
978-0-9719906-6-1

Copyright 2007 by Jack Webb
San Diego, California

All rights reserved. No part of this work may be reproduced or transmitted in any form by any means, except as may be expressly permitted by the 1976 Copyright Act or in writing by the publisher. Requests for permission should be addressed to:

Jack Webb
c/o *The San Diego Union-Tribune*
P.O. Box 120191
San Diego, CA 92112-0191

Professional and student poets featured in this anthology also read their poems at the 2007 Border Voices Poetry Fair. The Fair was presented by San Diego State University and *The San Diego Union-Tribune* in collaboration with the Border Voices Poetry Project.

Art Director: Leslie L.J. Reilly
Lilac Design Studio

Cover image from a painting by Dr. Catherine Yi-yu Cho Woo

Editors: Chris Dickerson and Celia Sigmon

Introduction, and biographies of featured poets: Jack Webb

Photos of the featured poets – Robert Pinsky by Emma Dodge Hanson. Adrienne Rich by Lilian Kemp. Steve Kowit by Mary Kowit. Catherine Yi-yu Cho Woo by Emi Ireland.

Dedication

This book is dedicated to the memory of

Dylan

beloved son of Sean and Leslie,
the equally beloved artist who designed this book

The morning glory blooms but for an hour
and yet it differs not at heart
from the giant pine
that lives for a thousand years

— Teitoku Matsunaga
16th-century Japanese poet

Where is He?
by Marcie Agpaoa
Grade 10, Morse High

Introduction 11
Acknowledgements 15

Major Poets

Robert Pinsky 20
Adrienne Rich 24
Steve Kowit 28
Catherine Yi-Yu Cho Woo 32

Student Poetry 37

Winter Poems

WINTER DREAM / Sean Yukawa 38
THE FEELING OF SNOW / Edna Gudino 39
EL NACIMIENTO / Silvia Rodriquez 40
SNOWY CHRISTMAS / Dallas Bishop 41
DECEMBER FIRE / Adrian Austria 42
THE BLACK HORSE / Paul Achee 43
I GUESS YOU LIED ABOUT BEING AN ANGEL /
Chelsea Warfield 44
CRUEL SHADOWS / Nicole Kubiak 46
THE TWO BLANKETS / Angie Garbo 47
ENGLISH BREAKFAST / Kayla Krut 48
FRIDAY MORNING IN JANUARY /Ana Peña 49
A BIRD'S-EYE VIEW /Talia Isaacson 50

GOLDEN WINTER SHINES / Allison Zohn 51
UNIQUE / Dianne Vitug 52
WHEN I WAS SIX OR SEVEN / Joe Hulett 54
ME, THE LAMBORGHINI / Genaro Rodriguez 55
THE CAT SITTER / Jacqueline Guy 56
TRIPLE SHADOWS / Alex Skvolygin 57
FEAR IS STRONG / Roberto Peña 58
BLUE DESPERATION / Erick Alvarez 59
NIGHT / Jewel B. Jones 60
BULLY'S HAND / Chris Thaodara 61
A LIVELY STILL LIFE / Erwin Pagtaconan 62
SMOKE FROM A BARN / Regine Reyes 63
SNOW BALLS / Danice Delossantos 64
LONELY / Miguel Montes 65
I, THE WIND / Carmella Selleneit 66
THE DARKNESS WITHIN / Miguel Montes 67

Spring Poems

MARCH / Daniela Troncoso 70
THUNDERSHOWER / Gabriel Luansing 71
THE EARTH OPENED / Alex Salomon 72
THE SHY GIANT / Anne Dettinger 73
THE MIND OF THE EARTH / Colin Smith 75
I AM A BOOM OF LIGHTNING RAINBOWS /
Tina Quach 76
A CHANT OF SCREAMS / Michael García 77

KABOOM! / Lance Turnham 78
POWERFUL LIGHTNING / Jordyn Bell 79
TRUTHFUL MOTHER NATURE / Emily Benzie 80
THE SUN'S GOLDEN PROMISE / Karly Hampshire .. 81
FROM MY WINDOW / Taylor McCabe 82
THE METAL SCULPTURE / Griffin Wheatley 83
MY MOM'S BIG MOUTH / Janelle Calderon 84
MIDNIGHT FIRE / Athena Mann 85
MY GRANDMA'S KITCHEN / Bianca Maldonado 86
UNCLE / Bryan Del Toro 87
I GIVE YOU / Julian Wahl 88
RAIN CLOUDS / Crystal Hernandez 89
MY BROTHER WAS A CHOCOLATE
CHIP COOKIE / Haleigh Gill 90
THE TRUTH ABOUT LUNCH / Amber Grantello 91
THE LIFE THAT CANNOT BE DOUSED /
Alan Gacias 92
MY GRANDMA'S HANDS / Vincent S. Viernes 93
MY FRIEND IS A BUTTERFLY /
Kiara Jasmin Miramon 94
KATIE THE KOALA / Kathy Le 95
MY HERITAGE MASK / Hafsah Mohamed 96
MASK OF SURRENDER / Marwa E. Qabille 97
ODE TO MY JOURNAL / Hafsah Mohamed 98
THE SECRET OF A TEAR / Darin Truong 99
THE SORROWFUL ESCAPE / Corrinn Fracchiolla ... 100
FALL UPON LOVE / Briana Harris 101
THE PROMISING WONDERS OF LOVE /
Marcelina Krieger 102
I'LL GIVE YOU / Anna Williams 103

Summer Poems

JUNE / Anndrea Torres 106
SHELF CITY / Nathaniel Pick 107
SUMMER GIRL / Gabrielle Nicole Meza 108
CIRCLE POEM / Anne Rinaldi 109
ELECTRIC WOMAN / Kiara Jasmine Miramon 110
LADY IN A PAINTING / Danielle Henry 111
CANDLE COOL / Kassandra Cassel 112
I WISH TO LEAVE / Andrew Harris 113
A WEIRD DAY / Jesus Reyes 114
MEMORIES / Alex Romo 115
RAINBOW FISH / Benjamin Lam 116
ISLAND OF WONDERS / Samira Shikh-Ali 117
MI CONEJO "MY RABBIT" / Abraham López 118
ODE TO STARS / Darcie Vargas 119
SUPPORTIVE SUN / Jessica Burlaza 120
MORE THAN I THOUGHT / Kyra McNatt 121
AUGUST / Edwin Camacho 122
THE FIREWORKS THAT NEVER GO OUT /
Gabriel Krut 123
BACK TO WHAT WAS ONCE "PARADISE" /
Baron John Lester C. Pableo 124
THE HAPPY OYSTER / Klarissa Nieblas 125
ROCHELLE / Ashly Bloxon 126

HORSES OF NEPTUNE / Caitlin Meng 127
MACAW / Justin Dimdiman 128
HOPE ISLAND / Preouphista Buasi 129
IMAGES OF PEACE AND BLISS /
Katheryn Bagorio 130
HOME OF THE TANGO / Gabriel Rosales 131
HOW I WOULD EAT A POEM / Michael Mitchell 132
FRUIT BOWL / Natalie Schmidt 133
A NERVOUS TRIP / Emma Burke 134
SHE LIVES IN THE TREETOPS / Monica Navarro ... 135

Fall Poems

A FALL DAY / Nick Watkins 138
SAYS THE INNOCENT HEART / Mya Anderson 139
MOSAIC OF COLORS / Alyssa Yoshitake 140
THE WIND / Bella Ham 141
INNOCENT LEAVES / Jessica Winkler 142
THIS TIME OF YEAR / Jordan Houri 143
INSIDE CIRCLE-HEADS / Joshua Shtein 144
EXACTLY WHAT I WANT / Shelby Barnhill 145
THE SHADOW OF DREAMS / Jody Miller 146
MY SANCTUM, A GOTHIC PLACE /
Veronica Stehlik 147
LONELY LEAVES / Brian J. Fleming 148

SHIVERING AUTUMN OF COLOR /
Annie Odelson 149
THE ONE / Enzo Serafino 150
NEW LAND / Erin Perko 151
I WOULD PAINT IT MY WAY /
Derrick A. Evalobo 152
THE BIG LIE / Carleen Anderson 153
FORGIVEN DREAMS / Jessica Cohen 154
JOYFUL AUTUMN / Ethan Anderson 155
HEART ON THE SIDEWALK / Taylr L. Hunter 156
THE FIRE BELOW / Thomas Zlatic 157
WHEN I TRAVEL INTO THE PIANO /
Lumy Amador 158
ODE TO MUSIC / Emily Williams 159
SHIMMERING LAUGHTER / Eva Ong 160
JOYFUL AUTUMN, COLORFUL MEMORIES /
Rogan McDaniel 161
FLYING / Zoë Dorman 162
MASK OF HARSH TRUTHS / Faisa Hassan 164
THE FABRIC OF AMERICA /
Katherine Deutschman 165
RAGE / Jesus Gonzalez 166
FIERY RED / Isaiah Chavez 167
TEARS OF A PUNISHED CHILD / Samantha Staab .. 168
TEARS OF A WEEPING SOUL / Evan Caplinger 169
AUTUMN'S PROMISES / Ali Hoffer 170
TRANSFORMING SEASONS / Larissa Kyle 171

Honorable Mentions 173

The Poet as Prince of Pirates

By Jack Webb, Director
Border Voices Poetry Project

 Like many people, I have a secret and guilty admiration of pirates – especially "Black Bart" Roberts, the greatest pirate of all time who captured more than 470 ships in a three-year career and who – ambushed by the sly and treacherous British navy – died astride a cannon, roaring his defiance, cutlass in hand, as his drunken crew lay bedridden below decks …

 Now THAT'S a poet for you – a man clad in a red vest, a red feather in his hat, shouting his welcome to ultimate Mystery.

 In the next few pages you'll meet a lot of poet-pirates, as well as pirates in training (some of them as young as 8 years old). A few of these talented buccaneers-of-the-written-word are famous, including former U.S. poet laureate Robert Pinsky and Adrienne Rich, known far and wide for her towering talent.

 Others may well be famous in a few years. Like Regine Reyes of Morse High School, who raises the pirate flag with her brilliant first-place poem "Smoke from a Barn." Here are the first few lines (you can find the rest inside):

> Whose dream does this belong to?
> If it were mine I'd be frightened
> despite broad daylight
> Trench-coated, derby-hatted men
> Floating, suitcases & umbrellas in tow
> lined like columns of chess pieces
> suspended midair like a still-life of snow
> I can hear their wispy murmurs …

Now THAT'S good! Stunning, powerful writing, and – if you'll allow me a moment of pirate-like pride – evidence that the thing I and my shipmates set out to do, 14 long years ago, is working.

What we hoped to do, to put it very directly, was to raise the flag for another way of looking at the world. We were profoundly dissatisfied with the limited rationalism of Descartes, the almost militaristic rationalism that had conquered most of the world and fostered the rigors of business management and Freud (placing people in inflexible boxes and implicitly denying the possibility of genuine creativity). We posited a more pleasing and liberating reality: that the Self is in a continual process of unfolding, that this mystery of the soul is reflected best in art, and most especially in the art of poetry, and that from this mystery of the unfolding self, these soul riffs, these unfolding worlds, comes everything of value – the greatest insights of scientists and artists and spiritual visionaries.

And so we brought poetry to the schools and the community, in workshops and at our annual poetry fair. We hosted grand celebrations at Cox Arena featuring Maya Angelou, reading her poems to a jubilant crowd of 7,500 (this happened twice); we broadcast weekly TV shows showcasing student poets and Pulitzer Prize winners, and we did many many other things. Oh, such huge expenditures of volunteer energy, such massive amounts of donated cash, laboriously gathered by grant-writing (terrible to recall, those tedious hours meditating on budgetary tables and institutional requirements, bad as salt-herring and hot salt spray on a British privateer).

But it was worth it after all, for poems such as this one:

Winter Dream

Through the bedroom window
I see little puddles like broken mirrors.
The trees are bald, their wigs all gone.
I can sleep a little bit longer, but not all day.

This time of year there are no birds
chirping like a chorus of people,
and the only way San Diego
can have snow is in my dream.
Then the trees will have a new wig,
but it will be white, and the snow
will laugh and dance like a white clown.

Sean Yukawa
Grade 3, Hearst Elementary
Poet-teacher: Celia Sigmon
Teacher: Jean Feinstein

That poem won first-place this year in the elementary school division. It's good, so good that by itself it serves as wonderful introduction to this swashbuckling book.

Welcome aboard!! You will find herein a gaggle of soulful shipmates, caring crew-members on a "ship of fools" dedicated to freeing the imaginations of children. Poet-teachers, donors, volunteers, students ... they offer you what they have. And it's a lot.

Acknowledgements

This book and the March 2007 Poetry Fair are the result of a collaboration between dozens of poets, teachers and organizations; special thanks go to those organizations and individuals who helped underwrite this book and the Fair. Among those who have supported Border Voices with both donations and encouragement are the Helen K. and James S. Copley Foundation; the San Diego Commission for Arts and Culture; the John R. and Jane F. Adams Endowment; the California Arts Council; the Szekely Family Foundation; Audrey Geisel and the Dr. Seuss Foundation; and the National Endowment for the Arts. The 2007 Poetry Fair is also supported by Poets & Writers, Inc., through a grant it has received from The James Irvine Foundation.

A hearty "thank you" is owed the Border Voices board: Janet Delaney, director of Community Relations, San Diego Unified; Danah Fayman, philanthropist and creator of the San Diego Arts Foundation and Partners for Livable Places; Joy Hanna, former board member of Friends of the San Diego Public Library; Carleen Hemric, who is also a board member for three other organizations: Greater San Diego Council of Teachers of English, the California Association of Teachers of English (CATE), and the umbrella Friends of the San Diego Public Library; Blue Robbins, SDSU cultural arts manager; Eugene L. Stein, director, SDSU Research Foundation; Anna Tatár, director , San Diego Public Library; Stephen L.Weber, president, San Diego State University; John Weil, financial planner and investment manager, and a member of several boards of directors in San Diego; Catherine Yi-yu Cho Woo, SDSU professor emeritus who served on the National Council for the Arts for both the first President Bush and for William Jefferson Clinton; Elizabeth Y. Yamada, a former partner at Wimmer, Yamada and Caughey landscape architecture firm and a former member of the San Diego Commission for Arts and Culture. Thanks also to Joan Schlossman Webb, secretary to the board.

We are also grateful to the coterie of volunteer administrators who kept everything running smoothly through hard work leavened with humor, including Chris Baron, who doubled as fair manager; Veronica Cunningham; and Chris Dickerson and Celia Sigmon, who edited the annual anthology. Thanks also to the judges who selected the student art and poetry for this anthology: Joan Bigge, Marion Day, Deni Down, and Border Voices board members Carleen Hemric and Joy Hanna. And a grateful doffing-of-the-cap to Seretta Martin, who oversaw and updated the Border Voices Web site, monitored the hotline, and coordinated activities with the 11 Border Voices poets who go into county classrooms throughout the year.

And a VERY special thanks to *The San Diego Union-Tribune* for agreeing to co-sponsor the project, and to publish student poems and artwork in the newspaper at the time of the fair. Members of the *Union-Tribune* staff have expended many hours on the project, and the following list is not exhaustive: Vincent DePalma, the ever-helpful and conscientious community relations representative; Leslie L.J. Reilly, the graphic artist who designed this book, the fair poster, and other odds and ends, delighting everyone, yet again, with her cheerful brilliance; Drew Schlosberg, community and public relations manager; Jack Webb, assistant news editor and founder-director of Border Voices; and Margo Raynes, who helped coordinate *Union-Tribune* efforts on behalf of Border Voices. Finally, we would like to express our deep appreciation to Karin Winner, editor of the *Union-Tribune*, for her continuing support over the years.

We also offer our deep appreciation to the 11 Border Voices poets who are currently going into San Diego County classrooms to teach the art of verse: Francisco Bustos, Brandon Cesmat, Veronica Cunningham, Gloria Foster, Jackleen Holton, Georgette James, Roxanne Young Kilbourne, Seretta Martin, Jill Moses, Johnnierenee Nia Nelson, and Celia Sigmon.

Following is a list of others who have contributed money, in-kind contributions, or moral and/or logistical support to the

Border Voices Poetry Project over the years:

The Administrators Association of San Diego City Schools; the Associated Students of San Diego State University; the Association of San Diego Educators of the Gifted; Barnes & Noble/Bookstar; Borders Books & Music; California Poets in the Schools; the San Diego Chargers; the College of Arts and Letters, SDSU; the San Diego County Office of Education, with special thanks to Richard A. Harrison, ITV production and programming manager; the Greater San Diego Council of Teachers of English; the San Diego Padres; and Kenneth A. Packer, General Book Buyer / Manager, Aztec Shops, Ltd.

Thanks, too, to the San Diego Unified School District, with special thanks to the Office of School Site Support, Instruction and Curriculum; and to Carol Osborne, director of the district's Department of Literacy. We are grateful for the help of dozens of other administrators and teachers in the district, and will pick one to represent them all: Sarah Sullivan, principal of Pershing Middle School, who helped the Border Voices Poetry Project organize and document one of its most ambitious programs – a full year of poetry workshops at the school, involving every student; with follow-up monitoring of standardized testing through 2004. And finally, sincere appreciation goes to the National School District and its staff, teachers and administrators for their many years of active involvement in the project.

Major **Poets**

Taking Center Stage … Guest Poets from the 2007 Poetry Fair

A NOTE TO THE READER: The biographies of our four Star Poets were taken, in large part, from "The Best of Border Voices," which also includes humorous essays, poems, and biographies of 26 other internationally acclaimed poets, as well as many other attractions. At the bottom of this page you'll find more information about this excellent book.[1]

---

[1] *The Best of Border Voices: Poet Laureates, Pulitzer Prize Winners & the Wisdom of Kids* by Jack Webb (editor), Hardcover, Illustrated, 328 pages. www.level4press.com ($24.95).

Robert Pinsky
1998 & 2007 Border Voices Poetry fairs
"All art is quite useless."
– **Oscar Wilde**

  Robert Pinsky loves language SO much: he savors its rough roots (the Germanic gutter-snarls and growls echoing beneath modern English) as much as he loves its soaring grace notes. It is this love that is reflected in the accompanying poem, which celebrates the endearing paradoxes of the language that binds and divides us ("That it is visible, invisible, dark and clear" and so on).
  What may not be immediately obvious, unless you step WAY back from the poem, is that it is also a very short tribute, an act of compassionate admiration for those who – although deaf and / or blind – can still achieve insight and art. It is thus a celebration not only of language, but of the heroism displayed by the fragile, which is all of us…
  And as such it gives the lie to the Oscar Wilde aphorism above, a much-quoted bit of nonsense uttered by the Irish playwright while he was in a VERY bad mood. When not suffering from an emotional hangover, Wilde was MUCH more forthcoming about the central role of art in guiding human affairs, noting that "Life imitates art far more than art imitates Life," and "It is through art, and through art only, that we can realise our perfection."
  It is an insight that is embodied in the poem printed here, and it is an insight that has apparently inspired Pinsky throughout his admirable and useful career as poet, professor and (from 1997-2000) Poet Laureate of the United States.
  It may seem odd to describe a great poet as useful – but in fact ALL great writing is useful, whether it be Plato's *Dialogues* or Shakespeare's plays – both of which

nourish wisdom as well as insight into human affairs. In the same way, Yeats' poems feed the imagination and sensitize the ear, while Francis Bacon's essays help us to think and live WELL ...
Pinsky's work is useful in just that way. A few examples (which is all we have room for):

(1) Pinsky's fourth book of poems, *The Want Bone*, dealt with the chameleon-like nature of the modern intellectual – his / her ability to adopt numerous personas and belief-systems, all of them potent, none of them absolute – and helped us see how to live with this purgatorial (and often exhilarating) uncertainty.

(2) While he was Poet Laureate, Pinsky was bombarded with requests to appear on TV shows and at various art events. He guided himself by what was useful. For example, as he told an interviewer for *Meridian* magazine: "There will be some things that just seem as though this is what the post was created for, something that involves encouraging somebody who's doing a very good job, bringing poetry into schools or something where you want to encourage and support something that's very worthy."

Robert Pinsky is the author of six books of poetry: *Jersey Rain* (Farrar, Straus & Giroux, 2000); *The Figured Wheel: New and Collected Poems 1966-1996* (1996), which won the 1997 Lenore Marshall Poetry Prize and was a Pulitzer Prize nominee; *The Want Bone* (1990); *History of My Heart* (1984); *An Explanation of America* (1980); and *Sadness and Happiness* (1975).

In 1999 he co-edited *Americans' Favorite Poems: The Favorite Poem Project Anthology* with Maggie Dietz (W.W. Norton & Company, Inc.). He has also published four books of criticism, including *The Sounds of Poetry* (Farrar, Straus, and Giroux, 1998), which was a finalist for the National Book Critics Circle Award; two books of translation, including *The Inferno of Dante* (1994), which received the Los Angeles Times Book Prize; and a computerized novel, *Mindwheel* (1985).

His honors include an American Academy of Arts and Letters award, *Poetry Magazine*'s Oscar Blumenthal prize, the William Carlos Williams Award, and a Guggenheim Foundation fellowship. He is currently poetry editor of the weekly Internet magazine *Slate*. Pinsky teaches in the graduate writing program at Boston University.

If You Could Write One Great Poem, What Would You Want It to Be About?*

(Asked of four student poets at the Illinois Schools for the Deaf and Visually Impaired)

Fire: because it is quick, and can destroy.
Music: place where anger has its place.
Romantic Love – the cold or stupid ask why.
Sign: that it is a language, full of grace,

That it is visible, invisible, dark and clear,
That it is loud and noiseless and is contained
Inside a body and explodes in air
Out of a body to conquer from the mind.

– Robert Pinsky

---

* "If You Could Write One Great Poem, What Would You Want It to Be About?" from *The Figured Wheel: New and Collected Poems 1966-1996* by Robert Pinsky. Copyright © 1996 by Robert Pinsky. Reprinted with the permission of the author and Farrar, Straus & Giroux, Inc.

Adrienne Rich
1996, 2004 & 2007 Border Voices Poetry fairs

A NOTE FROM THE EDITOR: In the 1970s and 1980s, Adrienne Rich was one of the brighter suns hovering over creative writing programs throughout the United States. Her ardent feminism excited women poets as well as sympathetic males. The way she so elegantly mixed the ghost of iambic pentameter with her free-verse excursions (as in "Diving into the Wreck") delighted those who hungered for form and musicality in poetry, while her intense concern with discerning what was of real value in our fluid society was an inspiration to all those struggling with similar issues – including the editor of this anthology. If anything, Rich's influence has increased in recent years. She continues to provoke hero-worship in many young writers, and to enrich all of us.

A SOMEWHAT-TRADITIONAL BIO: Adrienne Rich is one of this country's most distinguished poets. Her poetry is taught in English and women's studies courses across the country, and she is a revered teacher and activist. Since receiving the Yale Younger Poets Award in 1951, at the age of 21, she has not stopped writing in her distinctive voice, and in a language that incites action and provokes deliberation – about poverty, racism, sexism, violence, love between women, problems of survival, isolation and marginality.

One of her admirers, the much-honored poet W.S. Merwin, summed it up this way: "All her life (Adrienne Rich) has been in love with the hope of telling utter truth, and her command of language from the first has been startlingly powerful."

Rich is the recipient of numerous awards and honors: the 1999 Lannan Foundation Lifetime Achievement Award; the Ruth Lilly Poetry Prize; the Common Wealth

Award in Literature; the National Book Award; the 1996 Tanning Award for Mastery in the Art of Poetry (the Wallace Stevens Award); and a MacArthur Fellowship. In 2003, she was awarded the Bollingen Prize for Poetry.

She is the author of numerous volumes of poetry, including *Diving into the Wreck* (1973); *The Dream of a Common Language* (1978); *The Fact of a Doorframe: Selected Poems 1950-2001*; and *Fox* (W.W. Norton, Fall 2001). Her 2004 collection of poems, *The School Among the Ruins*, was honored with the National Book Critics Circle Award and was chosen as one of *Library Journal*'s Best Poetry picks of 2004.

She has also authored five books of non-fiction prose, including *Of Woman Born: Motherhood as Experience and Institution*; and *What is Found There: Notebooks on Poetry and Politics* (updated edition Fall 2003). Her most recent book of essays is entitled *Arts of the Possible: Essays and Conversations*. (W.W. Norton, 2002). She also edited Muriel Rukeyser's *Selected Poems* for the Library of America (2004).

In the fall of 2006, Adrienne Rich was awarded the Medal for Distinguished Contribution to American Letters by the National Book Foundation. The judges articulated this distinction as follows: "Adrienne Rich . . . in recognition of her incomparable influence and achievement as a poet and nonfiction writer. For more than fifty years, her eloquent and visionary writings have shaped the world of poetry as well as feminist and political thought."

She is a former chancellor of the Academy of American Poets.

Dreamwood*

In the old, scratched, cheap wood of the typing stand
there is a landscape, veined, which only a child can see
or the child's older self,
a woman dreaming when she should be typing
the last report of the day. If this were a map,
she thinks, a map laid down to memorize
because she might be walking it, it shows
ridge upon ridge fading into hazed desert,
here and there a sign of aquifers
and one possible watering-hole. If this were a map
it would be the map of the last age of her life,
not a map of choices but a map of variations
on the one great choice. It would be the map by which
she could see the end of touristic choices,
of distances blued and purpled by romance,
by which she would recognize that poetry
isn't revolution but a way of knowing
why it must come. If this cheap, massproduced
wooden stand from the Brooklyn Union Gas Co.,
massproduced yet durable, being here now,
is what it is yet a dream-map
so obdurate, so plain,
she thinks, the material and the dream can join
and that is the poem and that is the late report.

– Adrienne Rich

---

* "Dreamwood." Copyright © 2002, 1989 by Adrienne Rich, from *THE FACT OF A DOORFRAME: Selected Poems 1950-2001* by Adrienne Rich. Used by permission of the author and W.W. Norton & Company, Inc.

Messages*

I love the infinity of these silent spaces
Darkblue shot with deathrays but only a short distance
Keep of course water and batteries, antibiotics
Always look at California for the last time

We weren't birds, were we, to flutter past each other
But what were we meant to do, standing or lying down
Together on the bare slope where we were driven
The most personal feelings become historical

Keep your hands knotted deep inside your sweater
While the instruments of force are more credible than beauty
Inside a glass paperweight dust swirls and settles
    (Manzanar)
Where was the beauty anyway when we shouldered past
    each other

Where is it now in the hollow lounge
Of the grounded airline where the cameras
For the desouling project are being handed out
Each of us instructed to shoot the others naked

If you want to feel the true time of our universe
Put your hands over mine on the stainless pelvic rudder
No, here (sometimes the most impassive ones will shudder)
The infinity of these spaces comforts me
Simple textures falling open like a sweater

                                           – Adrienne Rich

* "Messages" from *FOX: POEMS 1998-2000* by Adrienne Rich. Copyright © 2001 by Adrienne Rich. Used by permission of the author and W.W. Norton & Company, Inc.

NOTE: Blaise Pascal (1623-1662): *Le silence éternel de ces espaces m'effraie.* (The eternal silence of these infinite spaces frightens me). See *Pensées of Blaise Pascal*, trans. W.F. Trotter, Everyman's Library no. 874 (London: Dent, 1948), p. 61.

Steve Kowit
2001 & 2007 Border Voices Poetry fairs

A Word of Explanation: The irrepressible Steve Kowit, having seen how Border Voices biographies are written, wanted to try writing his own. So here's Steve's "Bare-Bones Bio" and "More on Kowit," in which he ruthlessly dissects his own life. Our editorial comment follows immediately after.

BARE-BONES BIO: Steve Kowit is the author of several collections of poetry including *Lurid Confessions* (1983), *The Dumbbell Nebula* (2000), *The Gods of Rapture* (2006) and *The First Noble Truth* (Spring 2007). He is also the author of the popular poetry manual *In the Palm of Your Hand* and of the first anthology in America to feature the work of thoroughly accessible poets, *The Maverick Poets*. He has won the State Street Poetry Prize, the Atlanta Review Poetry Prize, the Tampa Review Poetry Prize, The San Diego Literary Lights Life Time Achievement Award, a National Endowment for the Arts Poetry Fellowship, and two Pushcart Prizes. He teaches at Southwestern College in Chula Vista.

MORE ON KOWIT: Steve Kowit came of age in the New York poetry coffee-shops such as Le Metro and Les Deux Megots, but that was also the era of America's Black anti-racist revolution and an essential part of his education. Formally, he studied in New York with two contemporary masters: Robert Lowell and Stanley Kunitz. He then spent a few years in San Francisco during the heyday of that city's counterculture revolution in the mid-60s. If Hart Crane and Walt Whitman had been his earliest poetic heroes, he came to see Allen Ginsberg and Robinson Jeffers as the guiding spirits of a new visionary and politically conscious poetics and populist, thoroughly accessible aesthetic.  After refusing to serve in Vietnam he spent three years living with his beloved wife Mary in Mexico, Central and South America avoiding the clutches of the genocidal US military. Returning to the States, he taught at community colleges in Idaho and Maryland, worked for a couple of years as a book editor in Florida, and then moved to San Diego where he became involved in the Gurdjieff, Vipassana and Zen communities. In response to being given the Zen koan Muji ("Do dogs have Buddha-nature") by one of his teachers, Kowit sat in meditation with the question for several months and then formed San Diego County's first animal rights movement. After years of teaching poetry writing workshops he organized his thoughts and prejudices on the subject into the well-known teaching manual: *In the Palm of Your Hand: The Poet's Portable Workshop*, which remains, many years later, one of the most popular books on the subject. In recent years, like a number of other politically conscious American Jews, he has become a vociferous advocate for the rights of the Palestinian people.

EDITORIAL COMMENT ON STEVE'S BIO: Good job, Steve.

UNOFFICIAL COMMENT: Steve left out that he is the sort of guy whose phone is always ringing off the hook with people needing advice or a shoulder to cry on or a friend to laugh with, all of which he is happy to provide. He ALSO left out how every page of his books, as the critic Ron Koertge said, "enchants or breaks my heart or makes me laugh. Or all three at once!"

THE BLUE DRESS

When I grab big Eddie, the gopher drops from his teeth,
& bolts for the closet, vanishing
into a clutter of shoes & valises & vacuum attachments
& endless crates of miscellaneous rubbish.
Grumbling & cursing, carton by carton,
I lug everything out:
that mountain of hopeless detritus — until,
with no place to hide, he breaks
for the other side of the room, & I have him at last,
trapped in a corner, tiny & trembling.
I lower the plastic freezer bowl over his head &
              Boom! —
slam the thing down.
          "Got him!" I yell out,
slipping a folder under the edge for a lid.
But when I open the front door, it's teeming,
a rain so fierce it drives me back into the house,
& before I can wriggle into my sneakers,
Mary, impatient, has grabbed the contraption
out of my hands & run off into the yard with it, barefoot.
She's wearing that blue house dress.
I know just where she's headed: that big

mossy boulder down by the oleanders
across from the shed,
& I know what she'll do when she gets there — hunker
down, slip off the folder,
let the thing slide to the ground
while she speaks to it softly, whispers
encouraging, comforting things.
Only after the gopher takes a few tentative steps,
dazed, not comprehending how he got back
to his own world, then tries to run off,
will she know how he's fared: if he's wounded,
or stunned, or okay — depraved ravisher
of our gladiolus & roses, but neighbor & kin nonetheless.
Big Eddie meows at my feet while I stand
by the window over the sink, watching
her run back thru the rain,
full of good news. Triumphant. Laughing. Wind
lashing the trees. It's hard to fathom
how gorgeous she looks, running like that
through the storm: that blue
sheath of a dress aglow in the smoky haze —
that luminous blue dress pasted by rain to her hips.
I stand at the window, grinning, amazed
at my own undeserved luck —
at a life that I still, when I think of it, hardly believe.

– *Steve Kowit*

Copyright © by Steve Kowit

Dr. Catherine Yi-yu Cho Woo

2007 Border Voices Poetry Fair

BARE-BONES BIO: Painter and poet … best-selling composer and Feng Shui practitioner … member of the National Council on the Arts from 1991 to 1996 … beloved scholar of international repute whose students nicknamed her "Mother Woo" – the list goes on and on. It sometimes seems as if Cathy Woo, whose parents fled the palaces of China following the revolution, must never sleep.

And she doesn't. At least, not much.

Cathy admits she only gets about three hours a night; she does most of her writing and painting between 10 p.m. and dawn. Her gorgeous canvases hang in galleries and museums all over the world, from Harvard to Tokyo, and she also wrote one of Asia's greatest hit songs: "Day by Day by Day, Blue Is the Sky."

Her poetry is quiet and persuasive, as are her elegant public readings. As she told one audience:

"I have a soft voice, like a child. But sometimes a soft voice says profound things. Let us hope so today."

A NOTE FROM THE EDITOR: It's 3:30 a.m., and I just got off the phone with Cathy Woo, who had a brilliant post-midnight idea for improving the fair poster and e-mailed me, telling me to call her RIGHT AWAY, or at least as soon as I got her message … which I did of course, since I'm up writing this book … and the poster is much improved … BUT there's food for thought here …

Perhaps it's Feng Shui (or if not that, some other mystical concoction of myths, herbs, stones and hope) that gives Cathy her seemingly inexhaustible supply of buoyant energy. I suspect it was that irrepressible energy that caused NEA chairwoman Jane Alexander to name

Cathy as an Ambassador for the Arts, back in 1996. And there's something equally magical about her deceptively simple poems, two of which she shares with you in these pages … "Split Pea Soup" and "Rocks."

For modern (or should we say "Modernist") readers of poetry, nourished on the verbal complexities of T.S. Eliot, Ezra Pound and James Merrill, Cathy Woo's poetry may seem a bit flat. But it is precisely that quality that gives them a touch of the Oriental, a sense of the merging of two cultures. It was, after all, the flatness of classic Chinese writing that inspired Pound to some of his more brilliant prosodic experiments. It was from the Chinese that he and other Modernists learned the evocative power of piling one understated image on top of another, until a complexity is revealed that is nowhere explicitly stated.

Pound stumbled across this technique while translating Chinese poems that became the groundbreaking collection *Cathay*. Nowhere is the power of this technique more apparent than in Li-Po's "The River-Merchant's Wife: A Letter," a poem about a village woman who falls in love with her childhood playmate. That much-admired and much-loved poem begins with these wonderfully understated lines:

> While my hair was still cut straight across my
>   forehead
> I played about the front gate, pulling flowers.
> You came by on bamboo stilts, playing horse,

You walked about my seat, playing with blue
   plums.
And we went on living in the village of Chokan:
Two small people, without dislike or suspicion.

Look for a similar simplicity, and gentle humor, in Cathy's work.

1. Split Pea Soup

Split pea soup
        One small can
                My love shared with me
So rapidly
      We drank
           Smiling
                Holding hands
                      From a
                            cracked
                                bowl
Before it leaked away ...

2. Rocks

Others
      Fished
           Fish
               While I
                    Fished
                         Rocks

They ate
      Fried fish
             As I watched

Tomorrow
        Their fish
              Will turn to
                    White bones

But my rock
        Remain always
                White stones

— ***Dr. Catherine Yi-yu Cho Woo***

Winter **Poems**

The Four Seasons by
Danicka Ullman
Grade 10, Morse High

Winter Dream

Through the bedroom window
I see little puddles like broken mirrors.
The trees are bald, their wigs all gone.
I can sleep a little bit longer, but not all day.

This time of year there are no birds
chirping like a chorus of people,
and the only way San Diego
can have snow is in my dream.
Then the trees will have a new wig,
but it will be white, and the snow
will laugh and dance like a white clown.

Sean Yukawa
Grade 3, Hearst Elementary
Poet-teacher: Celia Sigmon
Teacher: Jean Feinstein

The Feeling of Snow

Snow is a ballerina who dances, twists
and spins all around the stage of winter

Snow is an enormous cloud in the sky
fluffy, oval, oblong

Snow, cold as Cinderella's stepmother
Sweet like a summer vacation

Snow is as white as a dream
or my head when there's nothing on my mind
Snow...

Edna Gudino
Grade 6, Lincoln Acres Elementary
Poet-teacher: Johnnierenee Nelson
Teacher: Adriana Medigovich

El Nacimiento
inspired by "El Nacimiento" by Felipe Morales

I want to show you
a glorious bright moon
and white-barked birch trees admiring it.

I want to show you a small blue lake
rough brown ground
where a bull and sheep gather.

I want to show you three humans:
a naked baby on the bare ground
a shepherd and a woman seated on stiff rocks.

The newborn's body glows like the Northern Lights.

The woman wears a dazzling orange dress
a blue shawl covers her shiny black hair.

The shepherd wears an olive green gown
with a matching green opaque cape.

I want to show you "The Nativity."

Silvia Rodriguez
Grade 6, Lincoln Acres Elementary
Poet-teacher: Johnnierenee Nelson
Teacher: Adriana Medigovich

Snowy Christmas

Through the imaginary window
I see a soft blanket of Virginia snow
and the hoof-prints of horses that pass.
In my grandparents' living room
is a big green Christmas tree
that I picked out special and
an old oak cabinet with glass dolls.

This time of year there are no leaves
on the trees. They are naked and cold.
But I will always see the shimmering snow
that covers the old evergreens
and children playing in the white winter.

Dallas Bishop
Grade 4, Flying Hills Elementary
Poet-teacher: Celia Sigmon
Teacher: Marci A. Knoles

DECEMBER FIRE

You friend, you foe, the crayon of life.
A Phoenix rising from the ashes of death
your fire pierces the heart of many.
In the midst of war,
the rivers of blood,
the boom of the cannons,
the taste of death.
Restriction , hate, anger, fear
sizzling as it brands the mind.
Your aroma so sweet
yet deadly as a rose with its thorns.
Envelope me in your warmth,
envelope me in your death.
Fly high oh so almighty
and slam through the freedom below.
So bold against the white of December
screaming out its praises to the Christ.
Red you friend, you foe,
the crayon of my life.

Adrian Austria
Grade 10, Morse High
Poet-teacher: Glory Foster
Teacher: Carol Zupkas

THE BLACK HORSE
a cut up poem

Straw, feathers, dust--
Seed dazzled
Over the foot-battered blaze of the earth
And then I'd wander off
Down the open lane
These winter days
Have no end
Comrades
I regret to inform you
I thought we could hold back the sea
How far I've gotten
I don't know
If I knew the name of the black horse
Persecution would be no more
The means of production
Has no end
The night's half over
Light will soon be our host...

Paul Achee
Grade 10, Morse High
Poet-teacher: Glory Foster
Teacher: Mary Scanlon

I Guess You Lied about Being an Angel

Brownies are better
than cookies.
Paris Hilton may sizzle
like jalapeños,
but she's no superwoman.
Diamonds aren't forever.
Too bad it's only Thursday.
The fireworks she watched
with you
were destroyed by the circus
that came to town, uninvited.
I wanted to marry Maverick
from Top Gun.
It's a shame ducks don't
roller blade,
but I hear they disco.
Slam-dunks
and shattered pretzel sticks
have taken the place of
where we met under the
Papaya tree.
And now you roll in a stretch
limousine.
I guess you lied about being an angel.
Nobody could ever hide such
wings.

It's funny how big kids with
crayons
try to color outside the lines
and I wouldn't want to be
a puppy
once I reached full growth.
I'd miss the days when
wiggling and dribbling
were acceptable.
It's a shame how things
work out.
But darlin' I've got an idea.
Let's gather the clouds
and set off a volcano
because stars always steal
the show...

Chelsea Warfield
Grade 10, Morse High
Poet-teacher: Glory Foster
Teacher: Carol Zupkas

Two Wishes Are Better Than One by Jan Lim
Grade 10, Morse High

CRUEL SHADOWS

Hidden between the cruel words
The sorrowful pain of the poisoned world
The dark memories surround our imperfect minds
Rage creates the darkened voice of death and life
The hidden expression we fear deeply to express
The cruel shadows of our pain
Escape the unspoken boundaries
Burying us within
Our crazed bitter scars
Exploding through aching time
Walking through the murderous stones of fire
Of cruel violent anger

Nicole Kubiak
Grade 8, School of Creative and Performing Arts
Poet-teacher: Veronica Cunningham
Teacher: Linda Matlock

The Unidentified Soldier by Angelo Naz
Grade 10, Morse High

The Two Blankets

Two chairs, two blankets:
different, yet the same.
The blankets are there for a reason,
but each in distinct ways
confronting yet avoiding.

The colors, red and white, do not
mix or touch as they stare
at the other with mystery
and brutality.

They are not enemies,
just beautiful blankets
that could become
a comforter, a friend,
or even a protector.

They are souls with different
ideas and views that should be
shared with the world
but never will be.

They are ignorant.
They are unique.
They are every person
who goes upon this earth.

Angie Garbo
Grade 9, Ramona High
Poet-teacher: Seretta Martin
Teacher: Connie Mendoza

English Breakfast

You forgot your summer dress when you left, and
I cut it into little shining squares of ivory.
I used them to steep my tea, so they have
slowly stained brown, but I didn't think you'd mind.

I remember how I used to have to train myself
not to point out the similarities between you
and your father: the way you fold your napkin
in your lap, the way he looks up at the ceiling
when he drinks his tea.

It is Christmas 1982 and our heater coughs and dies.
We chew sandwiches of dark chocolate and graham crackers,
and you're grumpy because you don't like the cold.
You mutter, "I just want hot tea, Jesus,
is that so much to ask?" I hold you closer.

Kayla Krut
Grade 10, The Bishop's School
Poet-teacher: Brandon Cesmat
Teacher: Chad Bishop

Friday Morning in January

Fill me with frosty snow.
Drown me with working papers.
Bring me the light of a rainy day.
Blanket me with warm water
from the shower.
Drop your water from the clouds
that you made black, but
give me some snow I can play with.
Open your snowy door, so
I can float on
your warm August waters.

Ana Peña
Grade 4, Pauma School
Poet-teacher: Brandon Cesmat
Teacher: Chris Gill

A Bird's-Eye View

Through my bird's-eye window I see smoke
curling up from the chimneys far below me,
the puddles sparkling and shimmering
like little clusters of diamonds.
The world is like a great white ball,
the evergreens sprinkled with white frost,
the lakes lined with ice, and I see
little dots of children, ice-skating
and playing in the crisp air.

This time of year there are no mourning doves
softly calling out to you, "Coo, coo, coo."
But in my mind's eye, I will always remember
the way the bare trees dance back and forth,
beckoning me with their thin fingers
to come and dance, too.

Talia Isaacson
Grade 3, Hearst Elementary
Poet-teacher: Celia Sigmon
Teacher: Jean Feinstein

Bird Splashing in the Water by Gabriel Luansing
Grade 5, Lincoln Acres Elementary

Golden Winter Shines

Golden winter shines
black dangerous night
in the scary lumpy valley.

Burnt orange feathers
whisper gracefully about
the beautiful wings
of a hyper hummingbird.

Hollow pine scratches
in the powdered hot red clouds
of twilight hills
slowly climb the music.

Allison Zohn
Grade 5, Jerabek Elementary
Poet-teacher: Veronica Cunningham
Teacher: Phyllis Collins

Unique

Special, unique is
unlike another
unordinary
it's extraordinary
original, individual
tingles your senses
it's unusual
unlike you
who desperately tries
to do as they do
I say being the same
is boring
conforming
it's stupid, not fun
"Let's all be the same,"
says the moon to the sun
If we all dressed the same
walked the same
and moved to the same music
I think I'd go crazy
I'm pretty sure
I would lose it

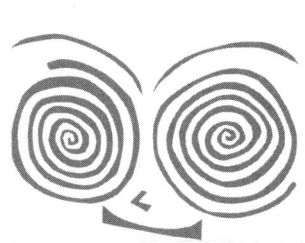

Swirly Blurry Makes Me Go Crazy by Diane G. Calata
Grade 10, Morse High

"Unique" is what defines us
It's what defines me
Unique is what separates
the stars
from the sea
"Unique ... being the only one of its kind."
like a snowflake that fell
from the heavens up high
I am different from you
as Earth is
from Sky
and I'll stay that way
until the day I die
You need to be different
you need to stand out
and being unique
is what it's all about...

Dianne Vitug
Grade 10, Morse High
Poet-teacher: Glory Foster
Teacher: Carol Zupkas

When I Was Six or Seven

Someone
moved into our house.

He loved to crack jokes
and tell stories
all the time.

His hair looked weird, like
two twigs I once found
under a tree. He made

my dad laugh and my mother
cry. He just sat there talking
all the time.

But it was easy
for me to make him stop.

I simply
turned him off.

Joe Hulett
Grade 5, Tierrasanta Elementary
Poet-teacher: Seretta Martin
Teacher: Jennifer Lench

Me, the Lamborghini

I am that shiny thing everyone wants but
not everyone can have. I can open my top.

You can show me off to your friends,
but I am the one who takes you wherever you want.

One day, someone had as much money as
you can imagine and he bought me with
a big shiny smile on his face.

Everyone can have me in their imagination.
Think of me taking you
where you've never been before at 190 miles-per-hour.

More of me are coming out, cooler and cooler,
in different colors, such as the sky on a shiny day.
Find me in your imagination.

Genaro Rodriguez
Grade 5, Pauma School
Poet-teacher: Brandon Cesmat
Teacher: Stephanie McEntire

The Cat Sitter

The cats upstairs are naughty.
They make such a racket.
And when I walk into their room
they're having a pillow fight
and trying on my pants.

Some knock over furniture
and lamps. Others play baseball
and jump on their beds.

But three cats are NOT
wrecking their room.

Mother cat, father cat, and baby cat
are cooperating with me.
They're getting ready for bed.
What a strange cat family.

Jacqueline Guy
Grade 3, Spreckels Elementary
Poet-teacher: Seretta Martin
Teacher: Deron Bear

My Cat Loves Cat Food by Satori Roberson
Grade 3, Chesterton Elementary

Triple Shadows

I have a shadow,
not one, but two
not two, but three
layers of shadows.
Oh, how there are three
of the shadows I see.

The first layer
is my shadow,
the one I always see.

The second layer
is the white and black shadow
that I am soon to be.

And last, but not least,
is the whitest shadow
known to be number three.

Alex Skvolygin
Grade 3, Hearst Elementary
Poet-teacher: Celia Sigmon
Teacher: Jean Feinstein

Fear Is Strong

Fear is dark as a bat's cave.
It sounds like a bulldog growling.
Fear looks like a bumpy frog.
Fear smells yucky like rotten meat.
Fear is strong!

Roberto Peña
Grade 3, Olivewood Elementary
Poet-teacher: Johnnierenee Nelson
Teacher: Monica Cho

Blue Desperation

Desperation seems black as a bear
and blue like a gigantic ocean wave.
It feels as hard as a brick.
Desperation looks like an old man
collecting cans.

Erick Alvarez
Grade 3, Olivewood Elementary
Poet-teacher: Johnnierenee Nelson
Teacher: Monica Cho

NIGHT

The waves of the ocean are like
A roaring tiger
Begging for meat

Jewel B. Jones
Grade 2, John Muir School
Poet-teacher: Roxanne Kilbourne
Teacher: Lindsay Hundley

Bully's Hand

The bully's hand,
a white stone when bundled up
with knuckles the size of rocks.

Under his skin, rough ridges rise
from punching walls many times.

"Does it hurt when you punch the walls?" I ask.
"No, never," he replies, faking a right.

Chris Thaodara
Grade 5, Marshall Elementary
Poet-teacher: Johnnierenee Nelson
Teacher: John Bartholomew

Stolen Fudge Bar by Pamela Sides
Grade 10, Morse High

A Lively Still Life
after art by Salvador Dali

Objects are not bolted to a surface
Nothing is meant to make sense
When it's morning it should be night
Have you ever felt the thrust of a knife
And seen a trail
Of glimmering lights
As it flies through the air?
Try watching a confused bird
As it tries to fly around
Notice the expression of paranoia
Constantly turning its head

Water is wild
Like animals
It does not like to be contained
A sea of blue
Is not an ocean
but merely an extension of the sky

When something is still
It is not frozen
It just moves in a manner
That nobody notices...

Erwin Pagtaconan
Grade 10, Morse High
Poet-teacher: Glory Foster
Teacher: Mary Scanlon

SMOKE FROM A BARN
inspired by René Magritte

Whose dream does this belong to?
If it were mine I'd be frightened
despite broad daylight
Trench-coated, derby-hatted men
Floating, suitcases & umbrellas in tow
lined like columns of chess pieces
suspended midair like a still-life of snow
I can hear their wispy murmurs
clawing, scratching past my minds' protective fog
Distraught, I attempt to flee from this over powering bog
Trench-coated, derby-hatted men
white dress shirts, black suits, ties
Floating midair before a powder blue sky
lined up, poised, with slight juxtapositions
An execution squad!
An impending invasion!
Foreboding, sinister,
like smoke rising from a barn
filling my eyes with melancholy
& my Psyche with bestial alarm

Regine Reyes
Grade 10, Morse High
Poet-teacher: Glory Foster
Teacher: Carol Zupkas

Snow Balls
a cut up poem

During the second grade
A time so far yet near
She stared out the window at something
Her first snow of the year
When the first flakes fell
She closed her eyes
And suddenly
A big surprise
She looked in the sky
Only the rainbow was there
Sunshine streaming
Reflecting off her hair
She went to the baseball diamond
To watch her big brother
His team was losing
Why'd she even bother?
Someone on the other team
Hit a grand slam
He dropped the bat and ran to first
Outfield in a jam
Had he been playing infield
He could've gotten the ball
They lost the game by seven points
And she's there all
By herself
During the second grade

Danice Delossantos
Grade 10, Morse High
Poet-teacher: Glory Foster
Teacher: Mary Scanlon

Lonely

Black
Is like the booming of the sunset
With the dancing stars
Next to the lonely moon.

Black
Is like a heart
In a dark cave
On a dark day.

Black
Is like the roar of a tiger
On a lonely mountain
On a cold night.

Black
Is like stars dancing
Around the cold moon.

Miguel Montes
Grade 6, John Muir School
Poet-teacher: Roxanne Kilbourne
Teacher: Joy Andrews

I, the Wind

If I was the wind
I would rush through
and make the palm trees
sway back and forth.

If I was the wind
I would play tag
with the tornado.

If I was the wind
I would make people so cold
they would stay inside
or wear many, many
layers of clothes.

If I was the wind
I would bang on peoples'
windows and doors
demanding to come in.

If I was the wind
I would play with rain,
thunder and lightning
during a storm.

If I was the wind
I would be annoying.

Carmella Selleneit
Grade 10, Morse High
Poet-teacher: Glory Foster
Teacher: Carol Zupkas

The Darkness Within

Cold night
Dark moon
Dark cave
No light
No way out

Golden sunset
Darkness

The evil darkness of loneliness
Takes you away from home
Takes you away from happiness

Miguel Montes
Grade 6, John Muir School
Poet-teacher: Roxanne Kilbourne
Teacher: Joy Andrews

Midnight Drift by Patrick Baun
Grade 10, Morse High

Spring Poems

JAQ
by Ryan Ancheta
Grade 10, Morse High

March

Drop me in the clear water passing through the river.
I will make the loudest ker-splash!

Bring me to the swimming pool where I can sink
down into the deep.
I will blow bubbles that look like the moon.

Fill me with the coming snow of Palomar Mountain.
I will shake myself in the wind so the snow can fall again.

Cover me with the flower blossoms of a spring evening.
I will grow into the apples that make the people happy.

Blanket me with the icy water from the waterfall.
I will splash the water up into a rainbow at sundown.

Drown me with spring's roses shining at night.
I will hold their stems in my mouth so they won't dry up.

Daniela Troncoso
Grade 5, Pauma School
Poet-teacher: Brandon Cesmat
Teacher: Stephanie McEntire

THUNDERSHOWER

Rain is a huge crowd
stomping their feet to the beat
Rain is a band of silver bullets
falling from the sky
Rain is a jackhammer
repeating a loud racket
Rain is a herd of zebras
sprinting away from their death
Rain is an old jeep
rugged and falling apart
Rain is a swarm of bombs
flying far and wide
Rain is a fireworks show
full of booms and bams
Rain is a stampede of wild bison
earsplitting stomping, charging
Rain is a tap dancer
tip tap, tip tap
Rain is a basketball game
swish, swish, slam!
Rain is a parade
it comes, but then, it's over

Gabriel Luansing
Grade 5, Lincoln Acres Elementary
Poet-teacher: Johnnierenee Nelson
Teacher: Adriana Medigovich

The Earth Opened

As a humongous volcano ripped open the earth, I popped out.
As soon as I came out people already knew who I was.
I melted the Earth to my liking.
I was all mighty.

I called onto the stars as my servants,
The moon my main advisor.
I ruled over all.

With Mother Nature I made the seas and the forests.
I created the animals of all kinds.
They were loyal with fear
Just to make sure they didn't turn into dinner.

I ruled the wind; my son gave me the weather,
I gave him the sun.
He ruled the sky; I ruled the earth.
Our family became powerful.

Every one of the four corners of the Earth knew of my greatness
From the Sahara to a kid's sandbox.
I was known
From the Pacific Ocean to the smallest puddle.
I ruled.

I was forever known . . .
As . . . a bird to the sky.

Alex Salomon
Grade 8, Harborside School
Poet-teacher: Jill Moses
Teacher: Kristine Schneid

The Shy Giant

I am the earth, as solid as a rock
and as gentle as new life.
I am night, as illusive as the stars
and as bold as the moon.
I am the ocean, as free
as the waves, as noble as the fish.
I am fearless as a soldier
yet gentle as a kitten.
But I also want to be a bicycle,
as hard-working as an engine,
or a cat, as secretive as a cave
and as quick as the wind.
But I am really a shy giant
that loves excitement.

Anne Dettinger
Grade 3, Flying Hills Elementary
Poet-teacher: Celia Sigmon
Teacher: Anne Lindsay

***Forgotten Eagle* by Jeronimo Tarango-Mims**
Grade 10, Morse High

THE MIND OF THE EARTH

At the gray sunrise,
the eagle of eternity gracefully flies
over a bare canyon
with a single palm tree.

The shimmering sunrise
reaches into the color-changing sky,
with wonderful nature
glistening with its ancient wisdom of hope.

The giant mountains just peek above the gentle
peaceful clouds
looking
at the monstrous,
beautiful
sky.

As the brown canyon whimpers
under the sheet white clouds' mighty power,
the more powerful sun
shines them away.

When the sunny day changes to sunset,
and sunset transforms to night,
the peaceful starts and the gentle moon,
look over the canyon of eternity.

The sunny mountains
whisper the lullaby of wind
over a lazy riverbed.

Colin Smith
Grade 5, Dingeman Elementary
Poet-teacher: Veronica Cunningham
Teacher: Rochelle Schwartz

I Am a Boom of Lightning Rainbows

I am a sonic boom of lightning rainbows
A glittery hummingbird
A crafty, brown rat
A dark shadow of empty thoughts
Wild about homework

A pineapple bonanza
Lost in the universe of creativity

A yellow mountain peak of joy
A racing river of wisdom
Bound in enthusiasm

A lovely bundle of meaningful memories
Traveling on a Jamaican sea of liquid blue

A tall, independent flamingo
A soul beyond wishes of light
Forever a bookworm
As sparkly as a gigantic ball of glitter

I am a sonic boom of lightning rainbows

Tina Quach
Grade 5, Dingeman Elementary
Poet-teacher: Veronica Cunningham
Teacher: Leigh Morioka

A Chant of Screams

Thunder
A large roar
A chant of screams
Of bitter crackling laughter

Thunder
A screeching volcano
An angry hot flicker and a roar of singing explosions

Michael García
Grade 5, John Muir School
Poet-teacher: Roxanne Kilbourne
Teacher: Stacey Kadlubowski

Surfing on Lightning by Jose Lopez
Grade 5, Lincoln Acres Elementary

Kaboom!

The thundering blade
Strikes the cloud
Ka boom!
As the dark moon crackles

Lance Turnham
Grade 2, John Muir School
Poet-teacher: Roxanne Kilbourne
Teacher: Lindsay Hundley

Starry Nights by Helena Stringfellow
Grade 10, Morse High

Powerful Lightning

Lightning is an electric outlet
that powers up our life.

It is a stingray
ready to shock you,

Very much an electric guitar
accompanied by the boom of thunder.

Lightning is a carnival with neon flashes
funky music, screams and laughter.

Lightning is a cheetah
traveling faster than a falcon.

Lightning is a chainsaw
chopping, downing trees.
Lightning!

Jordyn Bell
Grade 5, Lincoln Acres Elementary
Poet-teacher: Johnnierenee Nelson
Teacher: Adriana Medigovich

Truthful Mother Nature

A canyon's smooth whisper,
Holds sequoia truths.

The twilight hawk
Glides over
Mountain shine.

A sparrow wing
Sails over
Dawn's early break.

The maroon redwoods
Rained on
By glorious winter.

A sweet ladybug's lyric of spring
Sings through a setting dusk
Soft as a feather caress.

Emily Benzie
Grade 5, Jerabek Elementary
Poet-teacher: Veronica Cunningham
Teacher: Phyllis Collins

The Sun's Golden Promise

Hope drizzles
over the snowy mountain.

The crisp riverbed
laughs out
shimmering stars of glory.

A glistening sunrise
sheds laughter of moonlight,
for eternity.

The golden dove
seeks hope
at the evergreen valley
of forever.

A golden sunset
hides behind a sequoia tree
drizzling down
until it disappears
forever.

Karly Hampshire
Grade 5, Dingeman Elementary
Poet-teacher: Veronica Cunningham
Teacher: Rochelle Schwartz

From My Window

From my window
I see miles and miles
of apple green grass.

From my window
there are colossal
bright flowers.

From my window,
at the end of
the apple green grass
there's a little church
with a forest of trees
around it.

From my window
I see a mountain
with a path of tan,
gray and blue pebbles.
There are three huge
bushes on the mountain.

I wish I could come out
of my room
and reach the top
of the mountain
to touch the sky.

Taylor McCabe
Grade 3, Spreckels Elementary
Poet-teacher: Seretta Martin
Teacher: Nancy Chavez

The Metal Sculpture
after a photograph

The dark metal bars reflect the sun.
Some water is dancing, springing,
playing and having fun.
The garden is as calm
as the rocky path across the way
leading to a land of imagination,
calling, "Time to leave."
The garden of the future is like
a smart and small boy with secrets
and a knight in shining armor
waiting to bloom.

Griffin Wheatley
Grade 4, Spreckels Elementary
Poet-teacher: Celia Sigmon
Teacher: Peggy Araiza

My Mom's Big Mouth

My mom is like a clap
of thunder in the rain.
She talks and talks.
I can't even understand her.
I just hear blah, blah, blah.
Sometimes when she gets mad,
she cries like a puppy lost at night.
I only hear nag, nag, nag.
But I love her in my heart
and kiss her with my mouth,
though I don't let her kiss me.
I will always remember how
she loves black. Even my dad says,
"You always wear black."
But I love her.
She is my big-mouthed angel.

Janelle Calderon
Grade 3, Las Palmas Elementary
Poet-teacher: Celia Sigmon
Teacher: Myrna Kahle

Midnight Fire

A blazing fire
Against the horrible gray
Stormy sky
The icy cold
Like needles
Or a poison ivy plant
Then a tiny ladybug crawls
Out of a bush
Bringing hope to my heart
Then the voice of thunder sounds
After a lightning flash
It sounds like a competition
Between one flash and
The flash that follows

Athena Mann
Grade 4, San Pasqual Union
Poet-teacher: Brandon Cesmat
Teacher: Kris Conklin

My Grandma's Kitchen

White walls everywhere
with magnets of spoiled grandchildren
on the fridge
The smell of different spices
and chile cooking along
with meat, rice and beans
A window on top of the sink
with cigarette holders and a
picture of a Catholic saint on it
Everything's in a cupboard,
nothing out of place
A painting of the last supper
over the tiny wall that separates
the kitchen and the dining room
Mexican Cumbias coming out
of a tiny radio by the window
and if you pass by,
grandma grabs you
and starts to dance
like you were
at a party instead
of a kitchen...

Bianca Maldonado
Grade 10, Morse High
Poet-teacher: Glory Foster
Teacher: Carol Zupkas

Uncle

Uncle, you are like the clouds, lifting me up
into the sky with the twinkling stars.
You shine like the sun when you smile.
When you laugh, you sound like the earth.
I'll always remember that you live in the desert
but you move every two years,
that your house is like the inside of my heart.
You have made my world better
because you help my family feel better,
and when I cry you try to cheer me up
making my world funnier than ever.

Bryan Del Toro
Grade 3, Las Palmas Elementary
Poet-teacher: Celia Sigmon
Teacher: Myrna Kahle

Rice Cooker by Jeremy V. Ebidag
Grade 10, Morse High

I Give You

A mountain of joy to climb
An ocean of love to swim in
A universe of happiness to be part of
A planet of hope to live on
One person giving life to five
      Mom

Julian Wahl
Grade 3, Tierrasanta Elementary
Poet-teacher: Seretta Martin
Teacher: Bill Sprong

No More of Your Rainy Days by Aileen Mae Magsino
Grade 10, Morse High

Rain Clouds

The rain clouds
Cry of sadness
You can see their tears
Come down cold and stiff

The rain clouds
Cry of sadness
Their tears stream
Cold and stiff

Like snowflakes

Crystal Hernandez
Grade 8, John Muir School
Poet-teacher: Roxanne Kilbourne
Teacher: Simone Arias

My Brother Was a Chocolate Chip Cookie

My brother Alex was a cookie
with the sweetest chocolate chips.
He was a sea
of joy and love.
He was the night sky
shining down on me.
He was a wonderful miracle,
a dream.
He was the prince
in my world.
It was always an honor
to be his big sister.
Although he's gone
he will always be
a very unique baby brother.
That sea of joy and love
will always live
in my heart...

Haleigh Gill
Grade 3, Chesterton Elementary
Poet-teacher: Glory Foster
Teacher: Barbara Shekoufeh

THE TRUTH ABOUT LUNCH

Lunch is
Hustling freshmen for a dollar
Convincing the lunch ladies
They gave you the wrong change
Waiting the entire period in line
Because people cut in
Running to the bathroom
To clean up the soup
You spilled on your shirt
Copying a friend's homework
Only to fail the pop quiz
Walking all the way back to the cafeteria
Because you forgot a spoon
Rushing to decide whether to pick up
The cookie you dropped
Before your five seconds are up
Suspiciously looking around
As you drop the Cheetos wrapper on the ground
Sprinting to the fights
Faster than you run in P.E.
Hiding from your friends
Because you don't want to share your food
And
When the bell rings
You slowly trudge to fifth period
Lunch is over...

Amber Grantello
Grade 10, Morse High
Poet-teacher: Glory Foster
Teacher: Mary Scanlon

The Life That Cannot Be Doused
inspired by René Magritte

This painting shows a cloud
entering a building,
a building that's probably a home.
Beyond the slightly opened door
there is a light blue, clear sky
over an ocean and a beach.
The door is white on top
and wooden at the bottom.
The floor boards are wooden
and the wall around it is pink.
The inside of the house represents
something really ordinary, normal, boring and mundane.
After the cloud lets itself inside,
from curiosity or not,
the cloud changes the whole setting and presence of the house.
Since it came from the sky into the house,
it transforms the house.
The first sign of the change
is the door changing color.
Since the door has changed
the rest of the house will turn into a design
to match the door.
The cloud is life and brings chaos into this house,
to bring life where nothing can be doused...

Alan Gacias
Grade 10, Morse High
Poet-teacher: Glory Foster
Teacher: Carol Zupkas

My Grandma's Hands

Rough and jagged hands
plant seeds, water soil
grasp weeds
growing from the ground
Hands decrepit and idle
as a statue of cement
I ask, "Why do you work without rest?"
She answers, "I breathe for my garden."
Her hands also shuffle cards, cook food
Hands that crack at the touch
yet heal all wounds
My sympathy for her weaves
a shawl
yet she does not grieve
I look at her and she smiles
pulling weeds
forming endless piles...

Vincent S. Viernes
Grade 10, Morse High
Poet-teacher: Glory Foster
Teacher: Carol Zupkas

My Glass Half Full by Bessie Samson
Grade 10, Morse High

My Friend Is a Butterfly

I have a friendly butterfly
who is kind when she comes to visit.
She might seem fantastic
or weird eating macaroni
and cheese with me
but she also likes pollen.
And after lunch, her gorgeous
pink, purple and red wings
flap, flap, flap
when she flies home to her family.

Kiara Jasmin Miramon
Grade 3, Spreckels Elementary
Poet-teacher: Seretta Martin
Teacher: Millie Weil

Beauty by Lam Doan
Grade 10, Morse High

KATIE THE KOALA

lived close to Korea.
Katie loved to wear cute clothes
and to crunch kidney beans.
She was a kind hearted koala
who loved kittens and kangaroos.
She had a friend named Kate
who was a killdeer.
Katie loved to fly kites with Kate
and crochet with colorful yarn.

Kathy Le
Grade 3, Marshall Elementary
Poet-teacher: Johnnierenee Nelson
Teacher: Tara Malm

My Heritage Mask

Look at my chin
that bears the imitation of life.
Beware! My mouth holds back angry sharks
like people cheated of rights.
Listen. Do you hear the generations of joy and laughter?
Look into my eyes - bottomless
rain clouds, washing away pain and sorrow.
Then - an eagle in the darkness
and hope battles to ignite in the hearts of people.

You can call me the Mask of Heritage.

Do you feel the footprints of your forefathers
stamped across my face?

Hafsah Mohamed
Grade 12, The Charter School of San Diego
Poet-teacher: Johnnierenee Nelson
Teacher: Sumaiyah Vedder

Mask of Surrender

Gaze at my pointy nose.
I am the tent of surrender
a triangle of sadness.

Gaze into my fishy mouth
of truth and tears
wide as a valley.

Gaze into my thunderbolt eyebrows of death.

Look into my forehead.
See forgotten dreams soaring
soaring away.

I am the Goddess of Despair.

Marwa E. Qabille
Grade 5, Marshall Elementary
Poet-teacher: Johnnierenee Nelson
Teacher: John Bartholomew

Ode to My Journal

Your brimming pages
hold my darkest secrets.

When I'm filled with rage
ink flows, fast and hard.
My hands zoom across the pages.

When I'm happy, I write slowly
savoring the yellow feelings.

You are the backbone
my preserver.
You buoy my chaotic life
you ease my heavy heart.

When my soul aches with many burdens
your familiarity never ceases
to soothe me, old friend.

Hafsah Mohamed
Grade 12, The Charter School of San Diego
Poet-teacher: Johnnierenee Nelson
Teacher: Sumaiyah Vedder

THE SECRET OF A TEAR

It's dangerous when you have tears,
A fast-flowing river taking over your face
Winning the competition between good and evil.

Crying a tear is a burning droplet of falling water
Caught on fire
With a new adventure.

Sometimes, you explode with tears
Though you want to keep your tears a secret.

After your tears go away
You feel your strength coming back
Giving you the ability
To explore your peaceful life once more.

Darin Truong
Grade 4, Miramar Ranch Elementary
Poet- Teacher: Veronica Cunningham
Teacher: Cathy Kijak Tyre

Break the Silence by Reginald Paragas
Grade 10, Morse High

The Sorrowful Escape

Love reaches for
the softest whisper
of reassurance.

I think
peaceful love dances
with the lustrous moon.

Sorrowful love escapes
through the depths
of our souls.

Love always waits
for us
hidden in the depths of
our always-fearful hearts.

Corrinn Fracchiolla
Grade 8, School of Creative and Performing Arts
Poet-teacher: Veronica Cunningham
Teacher: Linda Matlock

Fall upon Love

I think dangerous love
dances
in a crazy state
of mischievous chaos
And I know
tender love escapes
precious time
in the loving eyes
of compassionate partners
I believe silent love
speaks,
yet not with simple words

Briana Harris
Grade 8, School for Creative and Performing Arts
Poet-teacher: Veronica Cunningham
Teacher: Linda Matlock

Cupid by Paulina Coleman
Grade 10, Morse High

The Promising Wonders of Love

Our promising love
dazzles all
who enhance our lives
and those
who mold our hopeful hearts
Silent love
empowers the confusing world
to live with one another
in quiet harmony
knowing that love unites
I think love
invites us
to acquire hope
and accomplish
our wildest dreams
and to reach our goals
for our happy lives

Marcelina Krieger
Grade 8, School of Creative and Performing Arts
Poet-teacher: Veronica Cunningham
Teacher: Linda Matlock

I'll Give You

I'll give you a picture
a camera
a lock of hair

I'll give you a matchbox
a donkey
a bowl of pears

I'll give you a book
a basketball
and a bottle of blue

I'll give you a flower
a river
a stream

and all of the things inbetween

I'll give you love
and memories of you
and most important of all, an old smelly shoe

Anna Williams
Grade 7, Harborside School
Poet-teacher: Jill Moses
Teacher: Cara Hetrick

Summer **Poems**

The Clouds Connect
by Alexis Flores
Grade 10, Morse High

JUNE

On the last day of June,
bring me some presents wrapped in red and black paper.
Drop me in the cool pool.
Give me a 90 motorcycle and
a blue and black helmet with
matching blue and black gear.
Open more trails on the rez so
I can ride fast with the wind blowing over my helmet.

Anndrea Torres
Grade 5, Pauma School
Poet-teacher: Brandon Cesmat
Teacher: Stephanie McEntire

Shelf City

I see half-fish-half-humans
playing guitars in the street.

Birds sit atop a lollipop tree.
Figures perch on skyscrapers
and bright colored lights dance
in the windows.

The scent of wood
hangs in the air. Tacos, chips,
horchata and tortillas sizzle.

The smells are wonderful
at the restaurant
where I am eating.

I hear church chimes.
Tourists dance on a tour bus
followed by a horse-drawn
truck with a cab full of chickens.

Yes, this city is wonderful.
But when I stop imagining,
all sounds stop, smells fade,

and all the clay figures
lie on the shelf
waiting to be brought
to life again.

Nathaniel Pick
Grade 3, Spreckels Elementary
Poet-teacher: Seretta Martin
Teacher: Daren Bear

Summer Girl

The girl's stockings are as green as a pea pod
cooling in a bowl.

Or green like summer watermelon
picked from a vine.

Her skirt is as red as a cherry.
So juicy.

The girl's blouse is as black as the blackberry
jam on her lips.

Gabrielle Nicole Meza
Grade 3, Tierrasanta Elementary
Poet-teacher: Seretta Martin
Teacher: Bill Sprong

Hibiscus by Jackleen Cuaresma
Grade 10 / Morse High

Circle Poem

They do not speak.
There is only the sound of his wings through the air.
The bat glows in the moonlight and everything else is jet black.

And as the opal was placed upon her grave,
The raven came and snatched it away.

On that one scorching day in the middle of the desert,
That last palm tree gave the scorpion shade before death.

And that one lonely hermit crab was dragged out to sea.
And that one lonely wave in the middle of the ocean held the crab close.
They were no longer lonely.
They were no longer afraid.

The poison dart frog taught the rose to be deadly,
And the little girl held the rose and pricked her finger on its thorns.
She bled.

Anne Rinaldi
Grade 7, Harborside School
Poet-teacher: Jill Moses
Teacher: Cara Hetrick

Electric Woman

The woman has electric hair.
Her face is colorful like a rainbow.
Her eyes are intense and red.
She is an Indian
in a whole different world.

It smells like smoke
sizzling everywhere.
Don't taste it,
you'll burn your tongue.
There's magic in this woman.

Kiara Jasmine Miramon
Grade 3, Spreckels Elementary
Poet-teacher: Seretta Martin
Teacher: Millie Weil

Lady in a Painting

She seems to have a blue foot
peeking out from the hem
of her many-colored dress.

Her festive skirt is shaded on one side
and light on the other.
A gold belt separates the two.

She is wearing a pink necklace, earrings
and a net that holds her flaming hair
away from her oval face.

I see keys held by a yellow, blue
and red chain, have fallen
on the floor beside her.
She seems to have lost them.

I am the person
standing behind her
whose face is green.

Danielle Henry
Grade 3, Spreckels Elementary
Poet-teacher: Seretta Martin
Teacher: Marisela Sparks

Candle Cool

The sea is a mystery to the little people on the hilltops.
If I bring jazz to the sea with the trombone I play,
then I will bring memories of love
to the sea creatures when they've lost it.

Remember, the world changes
like a fast-forward movie
by the press of a button.

A little candle burns on
the cooled lava.
Mother Earth pinches its light
with Her tree fingers.

When the candle slowly disappears,
the outside world is having the blues.

Kassandra Cassel
Grade 4, Pauma School
Poet-teacher: Brandon Cesmat
Teacher: Chris Gill

I Wish to Leave

I wish to leave this big town
and travel to tall redwoods
where birds sing and squirrels play.

I want to escape stress
leave smog behind
and live with sapphire water
and a diamond breeze.

I'd leave the sound of SUVs
and freight trains, to hear
the howling of a wolf.
        I wish to leave.

Andrew Harris
Grade 4, Tierrasanta Elementary
Poet-teacher: Seretta Martin
Teacher: Jennifer Lench

A Weird Day

The ocean shattered the peninsula
leaving mountains of diamond shaped land.
The lakes reflected the continent.
Frowning at the longitude and latitude lines,
the equator was shining from the Earth.
In the night it looked like a ray from the sun.
The cities' lights were outshining the moon and stars,
making the moon, stars and the shiniest jewelry look dull.

Jesus Reyes
Grade 6, San Pasqual Union School
Poet-teacher: Brandon Cesmat
Teacher: Lynne Anne Boulette

City by JiAe Min
Grade 10 / Morse High

Memories

I want to show you
a clock ticking
I want to show you
a boat sailing though gigantic waves
waves squishy and smooth

I want to show you
pebbles poised on a polka dotted scale
sand falling, time running out
a ship that sails away.

Alex Romo
Grade 5, Lincoln Acres Elementary
Poet-teacher: Johnnierenee Nelson
Teacher: Adriana Medigovich

Rainbow Fish

One day I caught
a rainbow fish.
It wiggled in the water
like a fast eel.
The fish sounded
like splats of rain
dropping from the cloudy sky.
I tasted the fish.
First I thought it tasted
like a tuna fish sandwich,
then it really tasted
like fried chicken.
The touch of the fish
is as slimy as a slithering slug.
Now it's time for me
to release my magic rainbow fish
back into the water.
Its colors blend like a sunset
blooming in the night.

Benjamin Lam
Grade 3, Chesterton Elementary
Poet-teacher: Glory Foster
Teacher: Barbara Shekoufeh

ISLAND OF WONDERS

Inside my heart is a place I can go to by myself.

Inside my heart is a beautiful island
with golden sand, emerald pearls
and a seagull that glides over an ocean
that sparkles like diamonds.

Inside my heart are palm trees
grouped like Hawaiian dancers
where the powerful wind
makes the sea of beauty move
side to side, back and forth.

Inside my heart is an Island of Wonders.

Samira Shikh-Ali
Grade 5, Marshall Elementary
Poet-teacher: Johnnierenee Nelson
Teacher: John Bartholomew

***Reflection** by Lea Renojo*
Grade 10 / Morse High

Mi Conejo "My Rabbit"
inspired by Iliana Fuentes

A big bright full moon
Sky dark, with no stars
Grass green as new corn
A white bright rabbit with long ears
Is running away
From something or someone
The colors around the moon
Are a brilliant aqua blue
The rabbit's tail and ears are hairy
But his body is sleek
I imagine the rabbit
Is trying to jump over the moon
He also looks tired
And has probably been trying
To jump over it for a long time
I also see the moon
Brightens the sky
This probably takes place in a park
With no trees only the green grass
The rabbit's wing-like ears
Make it look like he is flying
Looking for a place to rest
With his ruby red eyes...

Abraham López
Grade 10, Morse High
Poet-teacher: Glory Foster
Teacher: Carol Zupkas

Ode to Stars

The stars up above
shine so bright.
With no stars no
light would shine
ahead of you at night.
A star is like a dream
awakening every night,
a soul inside the star
watching you day to day.
A star is a great beauty
to the world, and having one around
is like having someone special near you.
Without a star,
there is no light at night.

Darcie Vargas
Grade 4, Kimball Elementary
Poet-teacher: Francisco Bustos
Teacher: Martha Robinson

Supportive Sun

If I were the sun
I would shine on you
so you would not be chilly.
I would smile at you
and give you heat
for your trips to the beach.

I would make your clothes
warm and dry.
I would be as hot as lava
or a pot of tea and as shiny
as an expensive crystal vase.

Jessica Burlaza
Grade 3, Marshall Elementary
Poet-teacher: Johnnierenee Nelson
Teacher: Tara Malm

Does the Sun Shine on Me? by Dan Angelo Surdilla
Grade 10 / Morse High

More Than I Thought

I am the sky, as blue
as a shining star,
and I'm also the day,
as light as an angel.
I am a river, as noisy
as a bird, or a car
as bumpy as a road.
I am a dog, as fidgety
and impatient as a wolf.
I am fire, as crazy as a horse
and as big as the ocean.
Actually, I'm more incredible
than I thought I was.

Kyra McNatt
Grade 3, Flying Hills Elementary
Poet-teacher: Celia Sigmon
Teacher: Anne Lindsay.

August

Fill me up with cake and
drop Henry in, so

we can stuff ourselves with
the chocolate frosted cake.

Lemon heads and suckers
will rain from the clouds.

We won't need an umbrella
just a bag to pick them up.

Call the bulldogs to
play drums at my party.

Take me and Henry
to Magic Mountain for fun.

Let monkeys make a mess
with all the food.

When our stomachs are too full,
fluff a pillow so we can take a nap.

Edwin Camacho
Grade 4, Pauma School
Poet-teacher: Brandon Cesmat
Teacher: Chris Gill

THE FIREWORKS THAT NEVER GO OUT

Normally fireworks go out,
they just shoot up and disappear.
I thought all fireworks flew and disappeared.

But when I looked at it,
it stayed there.
When I tried to look away,
it stayed.

Many people wonder why it stayed there.
But I know.

Gabriel Krut
Grade 2, The Rhoades School
Poet-teacher: Brandon Cesmat
Teacher: Molly McCorkle

The Mysterious Flower   by Karla Garcia
Grade 6 / Lincoln Acres Elementary

Back to What Was Once "Paradise"

When I was young
I loved to walk outside with my cousins
The color of the sky
Was blue and bright
Like a celestial utopia
With not a single gray cloud in sight
The weather was neither hot nor cold
But just right
My morning was fabulous
Like a paradise island
We rode bikes along the river
The sound of the river's current
Was music to my ears
A deaf person
Would give anything
To hear this silent symphony
Bringing satisfaction without a tear
This new sound made me sing
Although
The song I sang
Was out of tune and obsolete
But I sang it anyway
Even when it was time to eat
The sun was slowly setting
And time seem to wait
For the stubborn sun
But we were persistent
Kept standing in this beautiful
And unforgettable scene
When summer felt timeless...

Baron John Lester C. Pableo
Grade 10, Morse High
Poet-teacher: Glory Foster
Teacher: Mary Scanlon

The Happy Oyster

The happy oyster
is marvelous.
The shell is wet
with steam.
Water flows through
its open sides
as it rests on the beach.
It came from
a rock of white.
Time comes through
the water of shells.

Klarissa Nieblas
Grade 3, Spreckels Elementary
Poet-teacher: Seretta Martin
Teacher: Millie Weil

Rochelle

The limpet shell is like Rochelle
It has ridges on the outside
slightly rough from existence and environment.
On one side there is a hard shell
to block and protect
and the other side is soft and smooth
with vulnerability.
The outside is disguised to hide
the beauty and softness that lie within.
The outer shell is beautiful like Rochelle
with all its flaws
some natural and some from use.
On the inside is a sparkling pearl
white, bright, warm, and inviting
like Rochelle.
The outside is beautiful
though it may not be perfect
while the inside is like a precious gift
waiting to be discovered.
That's Rochelle...

Ashly Bloxon
Grade 10, Morse High
Poet-teacher: Glory Foster
Teacher: Carol Zupkas

Horses of Neptune

Neptune, god of the ocean,
comes thundering to shore
on his golden chariot,
roaring in, drawn by waves
of moonlit stallions.

Muscles rippled, their manes
bellow behind them,
each adorned with a necklace
of seashells.

Their webbed hooves
grab the air and their mouths
gap open as they strain
to bring their god to shore.

Some stretch,
others form arches
and recede back to the sea
to await Neptune's call.

Caitlin Meng
Grade 9, Ramona High
Poet-teacher: Seretta Martin
Teacher: Connie Mendoza

Macaw

Macaw, colorful as a rainbow
Flies high like the clouds
Many experiences
And many stories to tell

Red feathers, wings mixed
The vision of an eagle
And the beauty
Of a kiss in the rain

It can speak its own mind
Makes a beautiful song
And can make an old woman
Feel like a little girl

Flying to the west
Flying to the north
Soaring all over
To see the world

Imagine in your mind
And close your eyes
Imagine if you were a bird
Where would you fly?

Knowledge is power
And so is your mind
Take control and see
What you can find...

Justin Dimdiman
Grade 10, Morse High
Poet-teacher: Glory Foster
Teacher: Carol Zupkas

HOPE ISLAND

Inside my heart is an island
filled with cool breezes
the softest sand
and the smell of saltwater
salty like french fries.

The clear aquamarine water shifts
with the cold breezes.
The leaves, silky like a scarf
are as green as limes.
Someday, I will call the water
Ocean of Hope.

Preouphista Buasi
Grade 5, Marshall Elementary
Poet-teacher: Johnnierenee Nelson
Teacher: John Bartholomew

Island   by Latafale Aloese
Grade 10 / Morse High

Images of Peace and Bliss
after a still life by Lois Stecker

So many colors from satin blue
To patterned pink and purple stripes
Sharp, straight lines going in every direction
Figures splattered randomly
Cups of drinks and bowls of fruit
Juxtaposed abstractly
Pieces missing but filled with something else
Various colors in complexity
Unique shapes
A quiet subtle tone
And a sudden stop in time
With a pause on everything happening
Still and life altering
Images of peace and bliss
In a crazy atmosphere
Sounds of clatter followed by silence
Silence followed by nothing
All items fit into a vision
Of confusion and insanity
But perfectly in place

Katheryn Bagorio
Grade 10, Morse High
Poet-teacher: Glory Foster
Teacher: Mary Scanlon

Home of the Tango

Argentina
My mother's pride
An old house lost in nature's sweet cherry trees

Argentina
Castle of wildlife
At the Iguazú waterfall and river

Argentina
Native gauchos who dance the tango
And drink green yerba matte

Argentina
Mouth-watering steaks and currazcos
Reminding me of last red summer
With what seems to be long-lost family
Speaking Spanish with their famous *voceo* accent

Argentina
My family and my home

Gabriel Rosales
Grade 10, John Muir School
Poet-teacher: Roxanne Kilbourne
Teacher: Simone Arias

How I Would Eat a Poem

I will top the plump letters
____with Tabasco
and stanza by stanza let my ... mmmm
taste buds go
Every bite full of details and
delicious nouns ... mmmm
For sure this luscious poem
won't make me frown
I might even lap it up like
a dog
or even go ribbet and strike like
a frog
Maybe even chew & chew like
a horse
OH man, OH man, I know of course!!!
I'll get a verb, sit on the curb
let my tongue
SOAR!!!
With every delicious metaphor
I'll eat and eat
loading my mouth and mind with
punctuation
... mmmm watch out there's a Hot & Spicy
personification
I will top the plump letters
____ with Tabasco
and stanza by stanza let my ... mmmm
taste buds go ...

Michael Mitchell
Grade 10, Morse High
Poet-teacher: Glory Foster
Teacher: Carol Zupkas

Fruit Bowl

The round amber bowl sits
in my kitchen window.

A shiny red apple is the bowl's rose.
Three oranges are fruits of fire.

A lemon is the sun.
Ten blueberries form a lake.

I imagine them. In reality,
the bowl is empty.

Natalie Schmidt
Grade 4, Tierrasanta Elementary
Poet-teacher: Seretta Martin
Teacher: Jennifer Lench

A Nervous Trip

Through the airplane window
I see my house below, my friends
and family waving at me.
I'm going to Paris, France,
with Mom, Dad, and Evan.
This time of year, there's no telling
what's ahead or what we left behind.
But in my mind's eye
I will always remember the way
I threw my troubles out the window.

Emma Burke
Grade 4, Flying Hills Elementary
Poet-Teacher: Celia Sigmon
Teacher: Marci A. Knoles

SHE LIVES IN THE TREETOPS

oh amanda, pick an apple
'cause no one wants to see you
with your glasses on

your long brown hair's
got you climbing trees
and planting seeds
on your neighbors' sidewalk

strategic tears in your pants
have got me wondering
what you do with your nights

how about we sit all afternoon
and watch our breaths
living, momentarily, like us
in the cold wind's skirts

with the infinite amount of freckles
in the sky and on your neck
we'll sew you a sweater
and pretend we don't have outer layers
like the onions growing in your garden

no need for the fireflies
you keep in old glass bottles
during the day
we dance in their colored shadows
laughing on the walls with the sun
and wait for the night

Monica Navarro
Grade 11, Escondido Charter High
Poet-teacher: Brandon Cesmat
Teacher: Lori Soule

Fall **Poems**

> *The Kiss of the Wind*
> *by Janelle Celso*
> Grade 10, Morse High

A Fall Day

The wonderful season
Paints fallen leaves
Brunt orange
And fiery red.

Innocent autumn
Transforms memories
Into dreams of joy.

I think
Autumn leaves shimmer
Above the
Wonderful breeze.

Nick Watkins
Grade 4, Jerabek Elementary
Poet-teacher: Veronica Cunningham
Teacher: Kathleen Reid

Says the Innocent Heart

Corruption.
It fills the air we breathe.
Ignorance.
You inhale deeply.

Blink away
the promise
of yesterdays,
broken tomorrow.

Kiss away
the confusion of love.
Yearn for the tear
of a new hope.

A cold autumn
sings change
for the innocent heart.

Mya Anderson
Grade 8, School for Creative and Performing Arts
Poet-teacher: Veronica Cunningham
Teacher: Linda Matlock

Mosaic of Colors

Dancing Autumn
always promises
joyful gatherings
and lovely songs
of holidays

Summer chaos ends
and sleepy days
of glittering snow
begin

Guilty Autumn
transforms
Summer's warmth and light
into
Winter's frozen winds

Alyssa Yoshitake
Grade 4, Jerabek Elementary
Poet-teacher: Veronica Cunningham
Teacher: Elisha Templeton

The Wind

The wind is like a tiny whisper
that brushes against your face.
It listens to your problems
when you are troubled.
It may even answer
in a tiny little whisper.
Since it knows your problems,
it can solve your problems
which come and go like the wind.

Bella Ham
Grade 4, Flying Hills Elementary
Poet-teacher: Celia Sigmon
Teacher: Marci A. Knoles

Innocent Leaves

Innocent Fall sings,
With burnt orange leaves.

This golden season
Paints a burnt orange pumpkin.

Imagine then
The silver rain
      and golden skies.

Jessica Winkler
Grade 4, Jerabek Elementary
Poet-teacher: Veronica Cunningham
Teacher: Nancy Walters

This Time of Year

Through the car window
I see the jack-o-lanterns lit,
the witches cackling,
the ghosts haunting,
the skeletons singing,
the pirates stealing candy
from the Telly Tubbys.

Now that it's all done,
there are no monsters left
to haunt Halloween.
But I will always remember
the way the trees went bald,
and the mist in the moon.

Jordan Houri
Grade 4, Spreckels Elementary
Poet-teacher: Celia Sigmon
Teacher: Peggy Araiza

Inside Circle-Heads

I see problems going around in my head,
swirling and swirling.
I see majestic blue.
I see sparkling green.
I see tango orange.
I see numbers mixed up,
going in tornadoes around in my head.
I find circle-heads bouncing around the classroom.
I jump to the sky and find
tornado-swirl clowns making horrific mathematical jokes.

Joshua Shtein
Grade 5, San Diego Jewish Academy
Poet-teacher: Brandon Cesmat
Teacher: Cheryl Kolker

***Off-suited** by Alexis Pascasio*
Grade 10 / Morse High

Exactly What I Want

I want to be the sky
as swift as a cloud
or as dark as Halloween.
I want to be a river
and flow like the wind,
or be as straight and sturdy
as a bright red car.
I want to be a cat
and prowl around like a lion.
I want to be water,
as strong as Hurricane Katrina.
But I'm not big or small.
I'm really as medium
as a middle number,
and that's exactly what I want.

Shelby Barnhill
Grade 3, Flying Hills Elementary
Poet-teacher: Celia Sigmon
Teacher: Anne Lindsay

THE SHADOW OF DREAMS

The shadow of dreams is on my shoulder.
It controls my good dreams and my bad dreams too.
I asked it what its name is.
It replied, "My name is for me to know, not for you."
The shadow can be a circle,
but it can be a triangle too.
In my dream a boulder ran over me
and through the city.
I was blamed for the damage and
there was nothing I could do.

Jody Miller
Grade 5, San Diego Jewish Academy
Poet-teacher: Brandon Cesmat
Teacher: Cheryl Kolker

Ups and Downs   by Josh Poyaoan
Grade 10 / Morse High

My Sanctum, a Gothic Place

My room is my sad place
My room is my mad place
My room is the place
Where my life is faced

My room is where I dream
Where I hug my fat cat Sam
Where I escape the dishes
Where I store my wishes

My room is where I watch the leaves, leave
During autumn, my favorite season
My room is a bed, window, couch and a chair
And a black and white guinea pig covered with hair

My room is a sanctum
It is my lair
Where I dream ideas
That would make other kids stare

My room is where I keep secrets
and catch the light from the moon
It's where I'm true as the sunset
Where I can sing my own tune

My room is a gothic place
Where the sad servant escapes...

Veronica Stehlik
Grade 10, Morse High
Poet-teacher: Glory Foster
Teacher: Carol Zupkas

Lonely Leaves

When the lonely leaves
fall onto
the damp cold ground,
I hear the
tiny tap
they make.

With every hard step
a person takes,
I hear leaves break.

Brian J. Fleming
Grade 4, Jerabek Elementary
Poet-teacher: Veronica Cunningham
Teacher: Nancy Walters

Shivering Autumn of Color

Beautiful autumn, blasts us shivers
with its blowing wind.
Fall controls our abundant harvest
and layers of clothing.
Lively autumn promises to turn
our glorious warmth
into shivering cold.
Ancient trees paint wonderful piles
with their giving colorful leaves.
Warm leaves transform our dull ground
into a confused carpet of spicy colors.
Whispering fall,
the loud crunch of hurt leaves
under our feet
and joyful children saying
"Trick or treat."

Annie Odelson
Grade 5, Jerabek Elementary
Poet-teacher: Veronica Cunningham
Teacher: Jean Chalupsky and Guy Henry

The One

Through the misty window, I see
my dog running through the brittle leaves
crackling beneath her feet,
sneering jack-o-lanterns,
succulent turkey,
and the grass jeweled with mist,
the leaves moist in the early morning.

This time of year there are no trees
without a single amber leaf
except for the evergreens.
But I will always remember
the way my classmates yelled
and frolicked in the early-setting sunlight,
except for one,
the one who seems invisible,
never yelling, me.

Enzo Serafino
Grade 4, Spreckels Elementary
Poet-teacher: Celia Sigmon
Teacher: Peggy Araiza

New Land

Dark colors like black,
Sad times when no one was happy.
People scared and worried and not prepared
For things that are going to happen.
Dark red when people begin to harvest and
Start to enjoy life again.
No light colors, just dark and lonely colors.
Like a war is going on and all are sad and scared
And lonely.
It's like they are in a trance watching the dark blue
Waves break and listening to the black and gray
Cloud's madness and the eye-blinding yellow lightning
Voice roaring.
And I just sit there watching the people in their trance.

Erin Perko
Grade 4, San Pasqual Union
Poet-teacher: Brandon Cesmat
Teacher: Kris Conklin

I Would Paint It My Way

I would paint the future with two sides
One dark, the other light.
I would paint death as a way
of actually knowing you're alive.
I would paint happiness as nothing more
Than a bandage for sorrow.
I would paint a lie
As truth for the masses.
I would paint loneliness as the result
Of me wanting to be at all costs.
I would paint fear
As the teacher of staying alive.

Derrick A. Evalobo
Grade 10, Morse High
Poet-teacher: Glory Foster
Teacher: Carol Zupkas

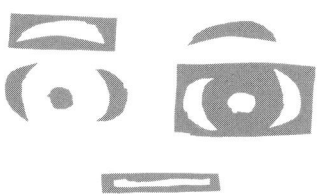

What Eye See   by Brady Balulong
Grade 10 / Morse High

The Big Lie

What is a lie?

A lie is what you tell your teacher
When you forget your homework
It's what you tell your parents
When something breaks
It's what you tell your sister
When you ruin her shirt
It's a mask for the truth
When the truth can't be told
It follows you around
Digging you deeper into the ground
It's hard to get rid of
But there is a way
Just tell the truth
The very next day...

Carleen Anderson
Grade 10, Morse High
Poet-teacher: Glory Foster
Teacher: Carol Zupkas

Forgiven Dreams

Imagine a midnight promise
of golden journeys
that await you.

The fall sings love
in all ways
of joyous holidays.

Blushing Autumn always promises
crisp burnt leaves
of flaming diversity.

Determination shivers
on cold Autumn's days
of windy dreams
that sing shivering songs.

Jessica Cohen
Grade 5, Jerabek Elementary
Poet-teacher: Veronica Cunningham
Teacher: Mary Wood

Joyful Autumn

Golden pumpkin season
Paints lovely
Innocent dreams of painful hope
With a sky of silver stars

Inspiring windy autumn
Transforms into
A cold promise
Of glittering happiness

Innocent golden nights
Sing a lovely song
Of hope
To the sleeping sun

Ethan Anderson
Grade 4, Jerabek Elementary
Poet-teacher: Veronica Cunningham
Teacher: Elisha Templeton

HEART ON THE SIDEWALK

I believe promising love kisses the bewitched foreheads of freedom, dreams and laughter. As we fall into deep sleep silent love dances through rivers of danger. And we all know the unforgiving world loves when the fountain of love runs dry.

The searing sun and calming moon merge, an eclipse of shameful love and hate. He asked me, "Why?" I usually don't leave my heart on the sidewalk but it fell out of my pocket that day.

Taylr L. Hunter
Grade 8, School of Creative and Performing Arts
Poet-teacher: Veronica Cunningham
Teacher: Linda Matlock

The Message by Torrey Curtis
Grade 3 / Chesterton Elementary

The Fire Below

The beautiful, brilliant flame burns,
sheens elegantly
in the midst of magical colors-
crimson red, dancing blue feet
shining brightly in the darkness.
The frisky flame cannot
live a life beyond its home.
The wick attaches itself,
never letting go.
The fire is born there
and must die there.

Thomas Zlatic
Grade 4, Hawthorne Elementary
Poet-teacher: Veronica Cunningham
Teacher: Ann MacDonald

When I Travel into the Piano

When I travel into the piano, I see the snowy
mountains growing more and more, as beautiful as the roses.
I hear the bell ring all around the schools, and the noise
sounds pretty to me. I feel that I am in a world full of birds,
  magic, plants
and animals, and I could watch other people discovering
this universe. I have already seen a lot of things, like you.
When I travel into the piano, I feel that it is
full of imaginary things.

Lumy Amador
Grade 4, Kimball Elementary
Poet-teacher: Francisco Bustos
Teacher: Martha Robinson

Ode to Music

Soothing to the ears like waves crashing on a rock
music relaxes your mind, your muscles
It gives you an adrenaline rush
a thousand knives stabbing you at once

Music heats your blood, your body
emotional music, like a teenage heartbreak
joyful music, like a baby being born into the world
Through music you can connect
to your soul, to your heart

Emily Williams
Grade 12, The Charter School of San Diego
Poet-teacher: Johnnierenee Nelson
Teacher: Sumaiyah Vedder

Keys to My Heart by Rubieanne Casem
Grade 10 / Morse High

Shimmering Laughter

Excitement paints
cornucopias of
thought.

Autumn sings songs
of imagination.

Autumn always promises
shimmering laughter.

Eva Ong
Grade 4, Jerabek Elementary
Poet-teacher: Veronica Cunningham
Teacher: Nancy Walters

Joyful Autumn, Colorful Memories

Windy autumn
Transforms a bushel
Of fallen dreams
Into the shivering autumn night.

Whispering autumn
Attracts burnt orange
Spirits of wonder.

Grey autumn
Whispers for the shivering rain
From the silent moon.

Autumn always promises
Golden dreams
Of magic to helpless people.

Rogan McDaniel
Grade 5, Jerabek Elementary
Poet-teacher: Veronica Cunningham
Teacher: Mary Wood

Flying

Out of nowhere my bed
started lifting
and the tan wood frame
trembled.

My purple comforter
was flapping
as I pulled it over my head.

Then the ride got smoother
and I pushed it
down under my chin
to gaze at the view below.

I did not see my room
or the beige rug
on my bedroom floor.
My house and city
were far from sight.

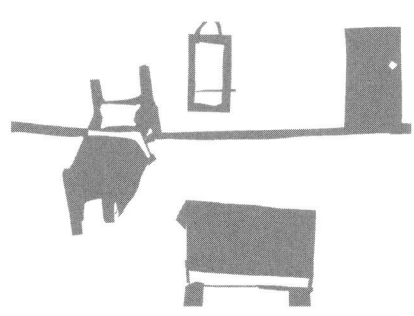

***Empty Room** by Alexis Lopez*
Grade 6, Lincoln Acres Elementary

When I floated down
the city was dark
and I saw news reporters
who took my picture
just as I landed with a thump.

It was time to wake up. I dressed
and went into the living room
where my dad was reading
the headlines.
    "Flying bed."
"Those news reporters are so crazy," Dad said.
    I laughed, "Really?
They might not be joking."

Zoë Dorman
Grade 3, Spreckels Elementary
Poet-teacher: Seretta Martin
Teacher: Nancy Chavez

Mask of Harsh Truths

Look into my flame-like eyes
You'll see a camp fire surrounded by Indians
my nose is like an upside-down bull with horns

Look into my sizzled face trying to be calm again
ready to charge
My mouth holds the unveiled secrets of fortune tellers
my eyebrows are like the tiny wings of a hummingbird
A diamond-like crystal lies between them
that points to harsh truths
I am the mask of anger and secrets

Faisa Hassan
Grade 9, The Charter School of San Diego
Poet-teacher: Johnnierenee Nelson
Teacher: Sumaiyah Vedder

The Fabric of America

Spectacular America
after the Constitutional Convention,
a brightly colored quilt, tightly stitched together,
each block representing
one of the new thirteen states.

Joyful, fascinated people in awe,
babies opening their eyes
for the first time.

But as time carries on,
the growing quilt makes room
for newer territories,
and begins to distort.

The aging quilt sags
under its own cumbersome weight.
And now, here we are,
with America, a dull, loose rag
in turmoil.

Katherine Deutschman
Grade 5, Hearst Elementary
Poet-teacher: Veronica Cunningham
Teacher: Chris Vasquez

Rage

Rage like a twisted tornado
rushing through my veins.

Rage like a rabid wolverine
biting my flesh.

Rage stinks like fresh vomit.
Rage stings like getting shot by a rifle.

Rage like Vesuvias with his mischievous glow.
Rage has the anger of two people in a fight.

Jesus Gonzalez
Grade 3, Marshall Elementary
Poet-teacher: Johnnierenee Nelson
Teacher: Tara Malm

FIERY RED

Anger, red like a scarlet red lobster
Anger sounds like a fierce dog barking at a burglar

Anger looks like a red hot volcano erupting
or a black cloud raining on me

Anger tastes like a dirt and rotten egg combo
Anger sounds like lightning hitting houses
and electricity lines popping

I feel angry when my brother hits me
and I hit him back

Isaiah Chavez
Grade 3, Olivewood Elementary
Poet-teacher: Johnnierenee Nelson
Teacher: Leticia Reyes

Tears of a Punished Child

The unforgettable tears
of a snake's venom
punishes you
With the unhappiness
of someone dying
you cry and cry
until your pillow is in a pool
with you inside
as a punished child
with the world
around you
saying to wake up
and be happy again
like you were
with that loved one
around

Samantha Staab
Grade 4, Jerabek Elementary
Poet-teacher: Veronica Cunningham
Teacher: Jean Chalupsky and Guy Henry

Tears of a Weeping Soul

Sparkling, salty tears
Running down my face in streams
Without a helpful hand to comfort
My weeping soul.

The tears increase,
Increase to a river,
To a rapid, agitated river
A river with no end.

Peacefully, my mourning
Tears stop.
A caring hand settles
My once weeping soul.

Evan Caplinger
Grade 4, Miramar Ranch Elementary
Poet-teacher: Veronica Cunningham
Teacher: Cathy Kijak Tyre

Autumn's Promises

Fall creates a soothing blanket of peach
settling over our soul.

Innocent, innocent autumn
transforms shimmers of light
into crisp shivers of wicked darkness.

Dreamy fall sings hopeful memories
into our quiet restless minds.

I try not to blush on a cool fall day
when the wicked wind blows
against my hidden fears.

The bright season of colorful autumn
paints burnt orange leaves and golden rain drops
on the cold, hard ground.

I blink frightfully on Halloween night
seeing the bright glow of the mysterious pumpkins
seeking my mortal soul.

The wonderful laughter of Thanksgiving
forgives my sorrow
throughout the confusing year.

Autumn always promises peaceful family gatherings
of gracious thanks
that heal the human world.

Ali Hoffer
Grade 5, Jerabek Elementary
Poet-teacher: Veronica Cunningham
Teacher: Jean Chalupsky and Guy Henry

Transforming Seasons

Rusty colorful
autumn transforms
into shimmering
windy winter.

Blushing pumpkins
rain a cheer of children's silly laughter
on burnt orange Halloween.

Raining, somber seasons
paint cold midnight dreams
within my colorful mind.

Larissa Kyle
Grade 5, Hearst Elementary
Poet-teacher: Veronica Cunningham
Teacher: Chris Vasquez

Honorable Mentions

Love Notes
by Dana Baniel
Grade 10, Morse High

Honorable Mentions

Chesterton Elementary

Joshua Fonseca, "Holding the Moon"

Dingeman Elementary

Kelsi Dantu, "Cherish the Moments"
Jenna Natrini, "Nature's Gift"
Jordan Taylor Potter, "The Heroes"

Harborside School

Alison Conover, "Ode to Old Jeans"
Eugenio zur Nieden, "The Poem Clock"
Genny Riber, "Connections"

Hawthorne Elementary

Emily Shum, "The Light's Way to Life"

Hearst Elementary

Kellen Gaughan, "Rusty Autumn"

Jerabek Elementary

Kasey Altman, "Solemn Seasons"
Lael Ceriani, "Fall's Feelings" and "What's Inside?"
Zoe Elliott, "What Is Golden Fall?"
Amy Gallagher, "Loving Light and Binding Darkness"
Ryan J. King, "Loving Colors of Autumn"
Sean Lapeyre, "God's Destiny of Confusion"
Steven Logan, "Mysterious Autumn"

Annie Odelson, "Tears from Me"
Alana Olson, "The Honesty Becomes Courage"
Emma Schopp, "An Unknown Whisper"
Jamie Smith, "From the Light"

John Muir School

Daisy Baran, "The Endless Ocean"
Pedro García, "The Strength of a Shadow"
Brian Robles, "Red" and "My Heart Makes Me Proud"
Alima Strickland, "Inside of Me"

Kimball Elementary

Andrea Rosales, "To the Beat of My Heart"

Las Palmas Elementary

Brenton Warren, "Papa Sun"

The Anti-penguins by Anthony E. Garcia
Grade 10, Morse High

Lincoln Acres Elementary

Perla Elizabeth Casteñeda, "Path of a Pearl"
Nicole Luansing, "My Preteen Life"
Manuel Zavalza, "To Understand Me"

Marshall Elementary

Fernando Bassoco, "A Good Day Begins"
Alisha Hing, "Frozen as an Iceberg"
Kevin Nguyen, "Kevin the Cardinal"
Helen Than, "Helen the Happy Horse"
Federico Torres, "If I Were a Racing Car"

Miramar Ranch Elementary

Annie Xu, "The Candy Sweetness of Sorrow"

Olivewood Elementary

Mario Azhocar, "Anger Feels"
Leonardo Carmona, "Sweet and Sour Wind"
Angel Carral, "Being Joy"
Dania Marie Villa, "Flying Loneliness"

Pauma School

Rogelio Caballero, "Saturday Morning"
Billy Espinoza, "March Ride"
Adan Hernandez, "Hold, Hit, Type"
Brandon Nelson, "July"
Georgie Nuñez, "Me, the Escalade"
Selena Payan Sanchez, "August"
Sofia Saavedra, "Spider's Legs"
Shawnee Schmidt, "What Shawnee Saw"
Michael Signes, "A Dog with Three Legs and One Eye"
 and "The Quilt's Cycle"

San Diego Jewish Academy

Max Abramson, "Fingerprints"
Yael Breziner, "To My Friend Meghan"

Davina Moossazadeh, "Bug Cars"
Adam Sloane, "Sandy"

Spreckels Elementary

Briana Aguirre, "Annoying Rat"
Renelia G. Bardales, "Angel Bird"
Kiara Gomez, "My Sister the Panda-horse"
  and "The Magic Painting"
Gerardo Gutierrez, "My Lovely Goose"
Jacqueline Guy, "My Mom"
Danielle Henry, "My Step-sister the Phoenix"
Amanda King, "The Giraffe"
Alexandria Knobloch, "The Beauty of Nature"
Dalton Longly, "Alien Sculpture"
Darian Maurer, "My Sister the Cheetah"
Abigail McGee, "Alex"
Gillian, Wright, "The Everywhere-colors Bird"

Tierrasanta Elementary

Bruno Arreola, "I Saw"

All You Got** by **Sandra Kaye A. Briones
Grade 10, Morse High